John Donne

Twayne's English Authors Series

Arthur F. Kinney, Editor

University of Massachusetts, Amherst

TEAS 444

John Donne, as a melancholy lover,
from the painting (ca. 1595) at Newbattle Abbey;
By kind permission of the Marquess of Lothian.

John Donne

By Frank J. Warnke

University of Georgia

Twayne Publishers
A Division of G.K. Hall & Co. • Boston

John Donne

Frank J. Warnke

Copyright©1987 by G.K. Hall & Co.
All Rights Reserved
Published by Twayne Publishers
A Division of G.K. Hall & Co.
70 Lincoln Street
Boston, Massachusetts 02111

Copyediting supervised by Lewis DeSimone
Book production by Janet Zietowski
Book design by Barbara Anderson

Typeset in 11 pt. Garamond
by P&M Typesetting, Inc., Waterbury, Connecticut

Printed on permanent/durable acid-free paper
and bound in the United States of America

Library of Congress Cataloging in Publication Data

Warnke, Frank J.
  John Donne.

  (Twayne's English authors series ; TEAS 444)
  Bibliography: p. 133
  Includes index.
  1. Donne, John, 1572–1631—Criticism and
interpretation. I. Title. II. Series.
PR2248.W28   1987   821'.3   86-27096
ISBN 0-8057-6941-2

Contents

Editor's Note

In this new brief but comprehensive survey of the life and works of John Donne, Frank J. Warnke provides a stimulating and compassionate discussion of the biographical events that shaped the work of English's greatest Metaphysical poet. By amending scholars and critics from Izaak Walton onwards, Warnke firmly places Donne back into the context of his own time and place, drawing on the baroque characteristics in his poems and prose and showing how the cynical, idealistic, and Neoplatonic strains complement each other in the widely read and widely taught *Songs and Sonets*. Warnke not only defines the techniques that Donne introduced to lyric poetry and meditative prose but redefines the "School of Donne" that followed him. All the major poems, such as the *Anniversaries* and *Holy Sonnets,* are given crisp readings and even the minor works—such as funerary poems and the prose of Donne's mid-career—are reviewed in order to assess most accurately Donne's contributions to the English literary tradition. This is a remarkably useful study, either as an introduction to Donne or as a reference guide to his work, which will be cited again and again.

Arthur F. Kinney

About the Author

Born in Massachusetts, Frank Warnke was educated at Yale (B.A.) and at Columbia (Ph.D.). Currently professor and head of Comparative Literature at the University of Georgia, he previously taught at Yale, the University of Washington, where he was chair of Comparative Literature from 1967 to 1975, and Queens College of the CUNY, where he was dean of Arts from 1975 to 1977. He has lived in Europe for extended periods, and has been visiting professor at the German universities of Munich, Münster, and Erlangen. His publications include *European Metaphysical Poets, Versions of Baroque: European Literature in the Seventeenth Century,* and an edition of the *Poetry and Prose of John Donne.* He recently published a volume of translations of poems by Louise Labé, Gaspara Stampa, and Sor Juana Inés de la Cruz. He is coeditor of *Seventeenth-Century Prose and Poetry.* His articles and reviews have appeared in many scholarly journals as well as in general magazines on literary subjects and also on opera. He is married to the novelist Janice Warnke.

Preface

John Donne is one of the great English poets and prose writers and, as such, has received a good deal of critical and scholarly attention. In the twentieth century especially he has been the object of sustained, probing, and often brilliant critical endeavors. Recognized from his own time on as an important figure in English literary history, Donne underwent a virtual apotheosis during the first half of the twentieth century, after Grierson's great 1912 edition of the poetical works, when a whole generation of critics and practicing poets (headed by T. S. Eliot) rehabilitated his reputation as a central figure in English poetry and as a role-model—both stylistically and spiritually—for modern writers.

The conception of Donne as a kind of modern man before the fact underwent considerable revision during the middle years of our century, as scholars focused on the specifically seventeenth-century aspects of his work—his links to medieval thought, to Renaissance science, to the larger currents of baroque culture, to the entire tradition of Western Christianity. The present study cannot hope to advance any new knowledge about Donne or any original view of his genius. Its more modest goal is to sketch an overview that will do justice both to his position as a man and artist of his time and to those peculiar individual features that led so many intellectuals of the 1920s and 1930s to regard him as a kindred spirit. In short, the attempted focus is on neither Donne-the-man-of-his-time nor Donne-the-man-of-our-time but on Donne the individual—one of the quirkiest, most passionate, most dramatic, and most original individuals in an extravagant age and in a national culture gifted with more than its share of eccentricity.

Another aim of this study has been to see Donne and his England in the larger framework of Europe in the baroque age. Unlike "classicizing" ages such as the Renaissance and the Enlightenment, the baroque cultivated irregularity and idiosyncrasy, and its artistic expressions are notable for their colorful variety. Hence, although it is neither possible nor desirable to draw detailed analogies between Donne and such Continental authors as Góngora, Quevedo, Marino, and Vondel, this study attempts to suggest something of the general kinship between Donne and his coevals. All were affected, inevitably, by the rich intellectual ferment of the seventeenth century. Donne's response to that ferment is one reason for the prominence given in this study to his *Anniversaries,* intellectually the most ambitious of his poetic works and the most revelatory of his reaction to the pressures of his age. No justification is required for giving major emphasis to Donne's *Songs and Sonets, Divine Poems, Sermons,* and *Devotions upon Emergent Occasions.* They are the works that have made him immortal.

The age in which we live, although it respects Donne as a classic, does not share the passion for him characteristic of high modernist authors and formalist critics during the period 1920–60. That relative falling-off in interest establishes a special need for this general study. For he has much to teach our age—above all, the lessons of wit, irony, and artistic sophistication.

Any scholar writing on Donne owes so many debts to predecessors that his/her work may be viewed as almost a collaborative effort. The Bibliography of this volume is, in effect, my list of acknowledgments. I must, however, record a special debt to the teachers who first brought me to Donne—to Alexander Witherspoon of Yale, Josephine Miles of California (Berkeley), and Marjorie Nicolson and Joseph Mazzeo of Columbia. I acknowledge also a gigantic debt to my friend and *quondam* colleague Louis L. Martz, *maestro di color che sanno.*

I thank my friend and coworker Marigene Banks, who typed the manuscript with skill, energy, speed, and intelligence. I thank my colleagues in the University of Georgia comparative literature department for providing aid and comfort in a variety of ways, direct and indirect.

Frank J. Warnke

University of Georgia

Chronology

1572	John Donne born in London some time between 24 January and 19 June.
1576	Father dies; mother remarries.
1584	Enters Hart Hall, Oxford, with his brother Henry.
1588	May have attended Cambridge.
1589–1591	May have traveled on the Continent.
1591	Studies law at Thavies Inn.
1592	Admitted to Lincoln's Inn for the study of law.
1593	His brother Henry dies in Newgate prison, where he was imprisoned for Catholic activities.
1596	Sails with English expedition against Cadiz.
1597	Sails with English expedition against the Azores. Becomes secretary to Sir Thomas Egerton, Lord Keeper of the Great Seal.
1601	Secretly marries Ann More, daughter of Sir George More.
1602	Marriage revealed; is imprisoned briefly, and dismissed by Egerton.
1603	First of twelve children born to John and Ann Donne.
1605	Travels in France.
1606	Takes up residence in Mitcham.
1607–1609	Makes various unsuccessful attempts to find suitable employment.
1610	Publishes *Pseudo-Martyr;* receives honorary M.A. from Oxford.
1611	*Ignatius His Conclave* in Latin and in English. "An Anatomy of the World" ("First Anniversary").
1612	*The Second Anniversarie.* Travels in Europe with his patrons, the Drurys.
1613	"Elegy on Prince Henry" in *Lachrymae Lachrymarum.*

1614   Member of Parliament.

1615   Ordained priest of the Church of England. Is appointed royal chaplain. Delivers first sermons.

1616   Preaches at court for first time.

1617   Ann Donne dies giving birth.

1619   Accompanies, as chaplain, Viscount Doncaster's embassy to Germany. Preaches at Heidelberg and at The Hague.

1620   Returns to London.

1621   Made dean of Saint Paul's.

1622   Several sermons published.

1623   Several more sermons published. Is seriously ill, probably with typhus.

1624   Publishes *Devotions upon Emergent Occasions*. More sermons published.

1625   Death of James I.

1627   Magdalen Lady Danvers dies.

1630   Becomes fatally ill.

1631   Donne's mother dies. Delivers last sermon (published postumously as "Death's Duell"). Dies on 31 March; buried in Saint Paul's Cathedral on 3 April.

*Based on chronological tables in R. C. Bald, *John Donne: A Life* (New York and Oxford: Oxford University Press, 1970).

Chapter One
Life and Career

Now that the twentieth century is approaching its end, we can see clearly how much importance John Donne has had for the literature and thought of our age. Great wit, poet, and preacher of the earlier seventeenth century, Donne enjoyed enormous esteem during his lifetime and for a generation thereafter, but critics in the age of Dryden and Pope, while admiring his wit, viewed his work with fairly strong neoclassical reservations, and the romantics—apart from Coleridge—ignored him. By the end of the Victorian period Donne had come to occupy a seemingly fixed position in the literary firmament—recognized as a force in the history of poetry and pulpit oratory, but condemned and ultimately dismissed for his extravagance and "tastelessness."

Early in the twentieth century, however, revaluation began. Rebellious young spirits—like the poet Rupert Brooke—found in Donne a poet who seemed to have more to say to them than did the dilute late-romantics of their own day. In an age—the Edwardian—that was beginning to find oppressive the attitudes inherited from the Victorians, Donne's frankness about sexual matters, together with his intellectuality, his colloquial manner, and his intensely dramatic confrontation of experience, was refreshing in the extreme. In the years before World War I modernism was emerging as the dominant literary movement in England, and Donne was destined to become, along with Baudelaire and the French symbolists, one of its patron saints. (Modernism was, of course, to be shaped by other hands than those of Brooke—dead at twenty-nine on his way to the doomed Dardanelles campaign. Yeats, Pound, and Eliot were to determine the course of English poetry in the first half of the twentieth century.)

In 1912 H. J. C. Grierson published his great two-volume edition of Donne's *Poetical Works*.[1] That event more than any other was decisive for the rehabilitation of the seventeenth-century master, making definitive and reliable texts available and placing them in a context of learned and sensitive appreciation. T. S. Eliot's immensely influential essay of 1921, "The Metaphysical Poets," created for the general reader an image of Donne that retained its currency for a half century and is still legal tender in some quarters. The essay appeared originally as a review of Grierson's anthology *Metaphysical Poems and Lyrics of the Seventeenth Century,* and the most resonant of Eliot's contentions—that the poetry of Donne and his fellows is free of the "dissociation of sensibility" that entered English poetry with Milton and has plagued it ever since—owes something to Grierson's identification of "passionate ratiocination" as the key element in such poetry.[2] If Eliot's appreciation did much to increase interest in Donne among intellectuals of the 1920s, it is also likely that Donne's "realism," his alleged lack of idealism, commended him to a generation disillusioned by the horrors and hypocrisies of the Great War.

The myth of the "unified sensibility" and the fusion of thought and feeling said to derive from it dominated critical discourse about poetry as a whole in Britain and America during most of the period between the two world wars, and it is probably accurate to say that the concept had a powerful effect on Anglo-American poetic idiom during that era. The myth created its own paradox with regard to John Donne himself: praised by Eliot for his possession of an artistic virtue lost to our age, he came to be seen as a model for emulation by twentieth-century poets and, hence, as himself a kind of twentieth-century man. He was often, especially during the twenties and thirties, exalted for his "modernity," and seen, as it were, as a tough-minded, hard-drinking, strongly sexed son of the Jazz Age.

Scholars soon attempted to redress the balance, to save Donne from being, as one put it, "kidnapped" by his modern admirers.[3] The picture of Donne the modern was challenged by that of Donne the medieval man, then as one in "flight" from medievalism, the Renaissance individual, the Elizabethan, the "Counter-Renaissance" man, and, with the growing popularity of such terms, as the baroque or mannerist author (we must not forget "Donne the Space Man").[4] The roles of seventeenth-century science, of French libertinism, of formal religious meditation, in Donne's sensibility were explored with great profit to our understanding of his work.[5] Even his "anti-Petrarchanism," a central tenet of Donne's critics and biographers in the 1920s, was challenged by convincing demonstrations of his profound debt to Petrarch.[6]

If the view of Donne's work was to some extent distorted by myth during the period between the two world wars, the same may be said of the view of his life and character. Donne's friend Izaak Walton had laid down the general lines in his biography (1640), which was the first of the poet. Walton's *Life of Dr. John Donne* is a glorious piece of English prose and a monument of sincere admiration, but it is, to be as kind about it as possible, unreliable. Living in an age in which the boundary between art and scholarship was more than a little fuzzy, Walton was as much hagiographer as biographer; he found in the life of Augustine a splendid model for that of his friend. We owe to Walton the mythical dichotomy between the piratical young Jack Donne—a love poet, rake, libertine, skeptic, and sinner—and the pious Dr. John Donne—sacred poet, preacher, exemplary Christian, and saint. The life and personality of the real Donne were less neat and more complicated, as well as being, despite their complexity, more unified. It has been demonstrated, for example, that much of his most passionate love poetry belongs to the later phase.[7] The edifying pattern of total conversion seems not borne out by the facts we know.

The Early Years

John Donne was born in London some time between January and June 1572, and he was to prove as dedicated a Londoner as Johnson and Dickens after him. He was descended on his father's side from a Welsh family whose members had fought for the Yorkist faction during the Wars of the Roses. John Donne the elder was a Londoner by birth and a prosperous merchant; he died when the poet was only four years old. The poet's mother was a Heywood—daughter of the dramatist John Heywood, sister of the Jesuit missionary Jasper Heywood, and granddaughter of the sister of the great Sir Thomas More. As this lineage indicates, Donne's family was Roman Catholic, and devoutly so: two of his uncles were Jesuit priests, and his brother Henry died in prison, where he had been incarcerated for harboring a priest.

Donne began his studies at Oxford in 1584 and he also, according to Walton, studied for a time at Cambridge, but he took no degree, his Catholic faith preventing him from swearing the requisite oath to the Protestant crown. By the early 1590s he was studying law at Lincoln's Inn in London, and during this period, on the evidence of some of his early poetry, he entered a phase of religious doubt, tentatively abandoning his Catholicism and adopting a freethinking position. He speaks of having initiated an intensive study of theology in order to satisfy himself about the opposed claims of Protestantism and Cathol-

icism.[8] It is clear, however—again on the evidence of the poetry—
that sober studies, legal and theological, did not consume all his
time. A contemporary recalls him as "not dissolute but very neat: a
great visiter of ladies, a great frequenter of plays, a great writer of
conceited verses."[9] Walton exaggerates in presenting the young
Donne as a great sinner, but it is clear that the poet was far from
celibate and, indeed, far from constant in his sexual behavior.

In 1596 the young Donne joined the forces of the Earl of Essex in
an expedition against Cadiz and, a year later, in one against the
Azores—experiences reflected in two of his early verse epistles, "The
Storme" and "The Calme." According to Walton,[10] Donne spent
"some years" in travel in Spain and Italy after the Azores venture, but
this dating is far from certain: he might have engaged in such travel
earlier. It is virtually sure that at some point in his youth Donne trav-
eled in western Europe and acquired several foreign languages.

In 1598 he became secretary to Sir Thomas Egerton, Lord Keeper
of the Great Seal. It is likely that by then he had become at least
nominally an Anglican. A promising career seemed to lie before him.
In 1601, however, he fell passionately in love with Ann More, niece
of Sir Thomas and daughter of Sir George More, Chancellor of the
Garter. Sir George had nourished quite different plans for Ann, and
Donne's imprudent clandestine marriage led to his dismissal from his
post and, for a short time, to imprisonment; his prospects for a brilliant career in public service were wholly ruined. Izaak Walton observes that Donne's marriage was the crucial episode of his life, and
that event marks the close of the first period of his artistic creation.

The Early Poetry

Donne's early poetry coincided with the last decade of the Elizabethan age, and the preoccupations of the early poetry are those of the
era—religion and sexual love. The writings of the youthful Donne—
the *Satyrs, Elegies,* and *Epigrams,* the earlier *Verse Letters,* the puzzling
verse narrative entitled *Metempsychosis: The Progresse of the Soule,* and at
least some of the love poems posthumously published as *Songs and Sonets*—concern these issues. A dominant theme of the *Satyrs* is religious: the persecution of the English Catholics in *Satyrs* II and IV,
and the question of which Christian sect possesses the truth in *Satyr*

III. (For Donne, as for his contemporaries, it was clear that, if one sect was right, all the others were wrong.) A powerful personal drama is implied within the *Satyrs:* the conflict between the urgent imperative to find and be loyal to religious truth on the one hand and, on the other, the powerful arguments of self-interest and, indeed, self-preservation. To be sure, Donne aspired toward success, fortune, and fame (difficult for an avowed Catholic to achieve in the England of Elizabeth) but, even more cogently, the informer-figures of *Satyrs* II and IV remind us of the ultimate price of fidelity to the old religion—a traitor's death (a very unpleasant death) at Tyburn. Still "unmoved thou / Of force must one, and forc'd but one allow; / And the right. . . . Yet strive so that before age, deaths twilight, / Thy Soule rest, for none can worke in that night" (*Satyr* III): the young intellectual's dilemma was not comfortable.

The religious preoccupation is not confined to the *Satyrs*. Although it is not possible to date any of the *Songs and Sonets* with confidence, some of them were surely written in the 1590s. With striking consistency, the imagery of the love poems is religious—as that of the religious poems (most of them later in date) is erotic. The poet seems compelled to find in amorous experience the transcendent constancy of the religious and, in religious experience, the immediate intensity of the erotic. Vainly, of course, but nonetheless insistently. Religion and sexual love were, and remained, for Donne the most important subjects in the world.

Among English poets of love, Donne is unique in the variety and complexity of his explorations. By turns cynical and impossibly idealistic, violent and ineffably tender, amused and exalted, he renders virtually all the contradictory moods a lover—in whatever time or place—may experience. Over the centuries learned commentators have tried to make sense out of this mad welter of expressed emotional life. One of the most popular critical ploys has been to posit a cynical and oversexed young rake who is transformed by the love of a good woman (Ann More) into an amorous idealist. Maybe, but the evidence has yet to be presented. More probably, Donne found the experience of love to be itself full of insoluble contradictions. Love between man and woman can be a source of profound and transcendent spirituality, but it may also stubbornly refuse to free itself of the body. It is here that Donne distances himself most decidedly from the majority of Petrarchan poets (although not Petrarch himself), as well

as from the facile oversimplifications of Plato that had acrrued to the
Petrarchan tradition. "Loves not so pure and abstract as they use / To
say who have no mistresse but the Muse," he writes, and elsewhere:
"Loves mysteries in soules do grow / But yet the body is his book."[11]

Although it is idle to attempt to find either a chronology or a narrative in the *Songs and Sonets,* something like a taxonomy may perhaps
be possible. (Parenthetically, it should be noted that the *Songs and
Sonets* contains no "sonnets" in the modern sense of that term. In the
second edition—1635—of the posthumously published *Poetical Works*
the term is apparently used in the older sense of "a short poem.")
Many of the lyrics in *Songs and Sonets* express a cynical or purely physical attitude toward love, and several of these (e.g., "Womans Constancy," "The Indifferent") praise inconstancy as a virtue. These
"outrageous" poems[12] (which are in many ways analogous to Donne's
youthful *Paradoxes and Problems* in prose) contrast sharply with those
poems—including many of the most famous in the *Songs and Sonets*—
that give eloquent expression to a conception of love that is at once
idealistic and passionate, aspiring toward an impossibly absolute constancy and a complete transcendence of the mundane. Exemplary of
this kind of lyric are "The Good-Morrow," "The Canonization,"
"A Valediction: Forbidding Mourning," and "The Extasie."

A third category of lyric, embracing a smaller number than the
other two, consists of conventionally Platonic poems (e.g., "The Undertaking") that present a view of love incompatible with either the
cynical or the idealistic. Some commentators have assumed that these
are poems of compliment, directed, like many of the *Verse Letters,* to
one or another of the great ladies who were Donne's patrons during
his years of penury. This assumption would imply a date of composition later than the 1590s; it is, in any case, as unsubstantiated as any
of the biographical speculation related to the *Songs and Sonets.*

The mood of the cynical love lyrics is paralleled, even intensified,
in many of the *Elegies* (so designated not because of any mood that is
"elegiac" in the modern sense but rather because of the meter in
which they are composed—iambic pentameter couplets, felt by the
Elizabethans to be the English equivalent to the elegiac distich of
Ovid). *Elegie* I is a dramatic monologue spoken by a brutally self-centered young man who is carrying on an intrigue with a married
woman. *Elegie* IV, "The Perfume," presents a similar figure involved
with a young woman whose father opposes the match, and *Elegie* VII

is the indignant outburst of a rake whose well-trained mistress has shown enough independence to reject him for another suitor.

Some of the *Elegies*—IX, allegedly addressed to Magdalen Herbert, and XVI, occasioned by a parting similar to those memorialized in the various "Valedictions" of the *Songs and Sonets*—belong almost certainly to a period later than Donne's youth. The *Elegies* have also been plausibly treated as biographical documents by many commentators. The sophistication of Renaissance and baroque conceptions of art—so unlike the naiveté of most modern conceptions—makes it difficult to be certain. Some of the *Elegies* may mirror the experiences of a young rake, others those of a passionate and faithful lover or of an affectionate friend, but they may also be viewed as experiments—both technical and psychological—in both the meter and the manner of Ovid's *Amores,* and in the dramatic and imaginative application of the philosophy of the contemporaneous French *libertins,* who held that the sole imperative of human behavior ought to be to follow the dictates of nature, unhampered by any prescriptions or by the prohibitions of traditional morality and theology.[13] (Later semantic transformations of *libertin* into "libertine" have, of course, contributed to the myth of "piratical" Jack Donne the rake.)

Metempsychosis: The Progresse of the Soule is a fragment, and a very peculiar one. Once again, religion and sex play the principal roles. In the most commonly accepted reading, this poem, which is based on the doctrine of the transmigration of souls, deals with the soul of "heresy"—incarnated (if that is the correct word) in the apple eaten by Adam and Eve, and, after a number of varied hosts, in the person of Elizabeth, queen of England.[14] Even though not meant for publication, the poem is obscure. The destinies of the heretical soul are accompanied by sexual adventures detailed with a realism analogous to that of some of the *Elegies*.

The Later Work

Neither at this point nor later was John Donne a professional poet—a designation that is perhaps, then as now, a contradiction in terms. But, with the destruction of his worldly ambitions through his indiscreet marriage, he was forced, after 1601, to turn to his pen to supply the needs of his growing household. (Ann bore him twelve children, seven of whom survived to adulthood.) The written works of the period 1601–15 fall into four categories: prose works of religious controversy ranging from the sober *Pseudo-Martyr* (1610) to the madly playful *Ignatius His Conclave* (1611); poetic works of an occasional or complimentary nature, ranging from verse letters addressed to various noble patrons to the complex and very great *Anniversaries* ("An Anatomie of the World"—1611—and "The Progresse of the Soule"—1612) in which fulsome praise of a patron's dead daughter magically triggers a rhapsody on the female principle and its role in the life of the spirit; one highly personal and deeply disturbing prose treatise—*Biathanatos,* or "a declaration of that paradox . . . that self-homicide is not so naturally a sin that it may never be otherwise" (not published until 1646); and, finally, work in the lyric genre—some certainly of the amorous *Songs and Sonets* and (as persuasively demonstrated by Helen Gardner)[15] most of the *Holy Sonnets* as well as several other of the *Divine Poems.*

His letters of the period give poignant evidence of the desperation that is at the root of *Biathanatos.* Recurrent illnesses in his family, together with constant financial need, are the themes of his correspondence. Sir George More had relented his harshness enough to provide his undesired son-in-law with a small stipend, but it was scarcely sufficient. Any dream Donne may have had of reestablishing a secular career was effectively crushed by, of all things, the admiration of King James I. The polemic brilliance of *Pseudo-Martyr* had convinced the monarch that Donne would be an ornament to his church, and he pressured the poet relentlessly to take holy orders as an Anglican priest—in the meantime seeing to it that all doors to secular preferment were closed. Donne hesitated—in part, no doubt, because of lingering questions about the identity of the true religion but also, it seems probable, because of a reluctance to exchange the bright worldliness of a courtier's identity for the holy drabness of a clergyman's. That such an attitude, so remarkably inappropriate for a professed Christian, was not uncommon among seventeenth-century gentlemen is indicated by Donne's poem "To Mr. Tilman, upon His Taking Holy Orders"—composed some years after Donne's own ordination—as well as by several passages in the work of George Herbert.

In 1615 Donne became a priest of the Church of England. In 1617 Ann Donne died, and the poet was left to enjoy alone his long-delayed prosperity. For prosperous he became: King James heaped honors upon him, the most signal of which was the deanship of Saint Paul's, conferred upon Donne in 1621. The literary work of Donne's final phase is predominantly religious and often somber. Definitive for that phase are the many volumes of sermons,[16] the great prose *Devotions upon Emergent Occasions,* and a good many devotional poems, including a few of the *Holy Sonnets*—the three printed from the Westmoreland manuscript in the nineteenth century. Of these, "Since she whom I lov'd hath payd her last debt" reveals the poet's inability to find religious consolation for the death of his wife, or to find in love of God an adequate replacement for the lost human love; "Show me deare Christ, thy Spouse, so bright and clear" indicates that, even as an Anglican clergyman, he remains in doubt as to the true church. Passion and doubt continued to haunt the distinguished divine.

A serious illness in 1623 led to the writing of the *Devotions,* a monument of baroque prose and of the tradition of meditative piety. According to tradition,[17] the "Hymne to God the Father" was also occasioned by this crisis, and Gardner believes that the "Hymne to God, My God, in My Sicknesse" was as well—despite Walton's assertion that the latter poem was written on Donne's deathbed.[18] Certain it is that from 1623 on the poet's thoughts were often upon death, to a degree extreme even in seventeenth-century Europe. It is not surprising that, seized by his final illness in 1631, Donne made his death one of exemplary piety. At his last appearance in the pulpit he delivered, according to Walton, "his own funeral sermon," and on his deathbed he donned his shroud and had his portrait painted in that garment. From that portrait a statue was later made, and installed in Saint Paul's.

Donne and the Baroque Imagination

The modern reader may find something theatrical about such a death, and may possibly be disturbed by the elements of showmanship and egotism in it. But the performance, if that is the right word for it, casts much light on Donne's character and art as well as on the baroque age of which both were products. "This is my play's last scene, here heavens appoint / My pilgrimage's last mile," he had written years before in *Holy Sonnet* VI (Grierson's numbering), rehearsing in his imagination the scene that in 1631 he was to play so well. The meditation on the scene of one's deathbed was one of the recognized subjects of formal meditation (cf. Donne's "Second Anniversarie," published in 1612, 11. 90–121), and meditation itself is, as Louis L. Martz has demonstrated,[19] a psychological experience that achieves its realization in dramatic utterance.

The dramatic, indeed the theatrical, is perhaps the major constituent of the baroque imagination. The seventeenth century is the great age of western European drama; the baroque lyric is partially defined by its dramatic modus operandi; and the great prose styles of the age, on the Continent as well as in England, are notable for their intensely dramatic quality. For Donne, as for Shakespeare, Sir Thomas Browne, Corneille, Calderón de la Barca, and a host of others, the venerable topos of the world as theater, the *theatrum mundi,* had an obsessive status—in life as well as in art.

To see the world as a stage is not to flee reality, or to compromise one's sense of it, but rather to find a means of engaging reality as fully as possible. As I have argued elsewhere, there are three major ways in which the relation of world and theater may be conceived: "the theater resembles the world" (this conception is, of course, the necessary basis for the existence of theater, and it is contained within the other two conceptions); "the world *resembles* the theater, and 'real life' often has an eerily stagey quality about it"; "the world *is* the theater, and the theater is the world."[20] This last conception asserts that neither one is more "theatrical" or feigned than the other, for in a phenomenal world of illusory appearance all is theater that is not God, and God finally has the combined functions of playwright, stage director, and audience. This conception—theater-is-world and world-is-theater—dominates and virtually defines the baroque imagination.

The theater topos explains much about Donne's life as well as about his death. It explains, for example, the strong element of role playing in the *Elegies* and elsewhere, as it explains the strongly dramatic cast of virtually all the lyrics, profane and sacred alike. It casts light as well on a paradoxical claim in one of Donne's letters: "I did best when I had least truth for my subjects."[21] Martz's notion of the relationship between the formal meditation and the creation of the self as a character on the stage of an internal drama is epitomized in the *Devotions upon Emergent Occasions,* in which the phases of the poet's illness become a series of dramatic encounters.

The final act had been played, and the poet-actor was in his grave. His contemporaries had been suitably edified by the entire life-performance, as the concluding words of Walton's biography, eloquently testify: "He was earnest and unwearied in the search of knowledge, with which his vigorous soul is now satisfied, and employed in a continual praise of that God that first breathed it into his active body: that body, which once was a temple of the Holy Ghost, and is now become a small quantity of Christian dust:—But I shall see it re-animated."[22]

Chapter Two
Baroque Europe and England

In his personality, his thought, and his art, John Donne was very much a man of his age. The European baroque period extended from approximately 1580 to approximately 1680 (somewhat later in eastern Europe), and it was notable for the extravagance, psychological tension, theatricality, eccentricity, and originality of its creations (in all artistic media), as well as for the quirkiness and intricacy of its thought.

The age may be seen as beginning with the *Essais* of Montaigne and the *Gerusalemme liberata* of Tasso, both in the early 1580s; the works are related stylistically but are worlds apart in the attitudes and values to which they give expression. In a certain sense they may be seen as prefiguring the two major directions baroque literary art was to take. In his epic masterpiece Tasso does not so much reject or react against the norms of Renaissance literature as intensify and modify certain of them to the point at which they become constituents of a new period style. Thus, the clear visual imagination and the aesthetic distance of Ariosto are transformed into a version of reality marked by extravagantly vivid coloration, indistinct or distorted outline, and a consistent saturation of image by emotion.[1] Tasso thus points the way toward the kind of baroque developed during the seventeenth century by such poets as Marino in Italy, Góngora in Spain, D'Aubigné in France, Vondel in Holland, Gryphius in Germany, and Giles Fletcher and Crashaw in England—the kind of style that some commentators have labeled "High Baroque."[2]

The achievement of Montaigne is marked by very different features. Both his style and his weltanschauung constitute a turning away from Renaissance norms in the direction of a wholly new set of conceptions. His skepticism and his resolute individualism are revealed as much in his manner of saying as in what he says: the impulse to *peindre le passage,* to portray the evanescent moments in which the mind does its thinking, constitutes a rejection not only of Ciceronian prose style but indeed of the entire Renaissance tradition of rhetorical, oratorical writing. Renaissance authors had presented—as persuasively or ornamentally as possible—ideas, arguments, postures, fictions, or spectacles already predetermined and, as it were, outlined; the *Essais* of Montaigne present—or feign to present—the thoughts in the process of being formed, with the consequent development of an asymmetrical, nervous, eccentric, and dramatically immediate prose. He is the earliest representative of the other great style of baroque literature (in prose and poetry alike), one that might be labeled "Metaphysical" or "Mannerist,"[3] which included among its practitioners Quevedo in Spain, Théophile de Viau in France, Constantijn Huygens in Holland, and Paul Fleming in Germany. His example was not lost in England, as demonstrated by the varied achievements of Bacon, Shakespeare, and John Donne.

Sources of Baroque

A major shift in literary style thus occurred in Europe around the turn of the sixteenth and seventeenth centuries—in the 1580s in Italy and France, in the 1590s in Spain and England, later still in Holland, the German-speaking world, and the cultures of northern and eastern Europe. The causes of this shift cannot be determined with any certainty, but a number of conditions may be significant. Among the factors that have been cited to explain the appearance of the baroque style, or styles are: the impact of the new sciences, particularly astronomy; the influence of a heightened and highly partisan religious sensibility; new conceptions in poetics; and intensified concerns with time and with dramatic relationships.[4] But, as I have noted elsewhere, there are some problems associated with any simplified causal explanation.[5] To find the roots of any period style in philosophical, scientific, or religious ideas, to locate such roots, in short, in extraliterary phenomena, is to risk an unprovable assertion. How can one be sure that such phenomena have *caused* the literary style? Can it be plausibly established that the stylistic innovations in question would *not* have occurred in the absence of the stated extraliterary stimuli? On the other hand, to explain the causes in terms of poetics or literary technique seems tautological: Are theory and technique not themselves parts of the style that is to be explained?

While recognizing that content and to some extent even specific traits of style are *conditioned* by extraliterary factors, one should bear in mind that a specific literary period is also the product of forces within literary history itself. The transition from the Renaissance to the baroque style seems to reflect the curious systole and diastole in Western literature in terms of which an age of classicism will be followed by an age of anticlassicism or, in E. R. Curtius's sense, an age of mannerism.[6] In any culture, after a certain range of artistic values, a certain set of norms, has been cultivated for some time, a point of saturation is reached, and eventually a sense of other values, which lie outside the reach of the established style and are clamoring for expression, makes itself felt. At such a point, energetic young writers appear and formulate a new style to give expression to the neglected values. The subsequent exploration of the previously neglected range of experience constitutes the literary period.

The literature of Donne's England participates fully in both the intellectual concerns and the literary historical rhythms of baroque Europe. One of the boldest of baroque thinkers, the Italian Giordano Bruno, spent a number of years in England in the late sixteenth century before returning to his inhospitable native land, where he was burned at the stake in 1600. He aroused the admiration of Sir Philip Sidney and others of the Sidney circle, and his ideas—about the infinity of created worlds and about the possibility of an heroic poetry based on intellectual passion—were widely discussed. Such names as Gilbert and Harvey may stand as exemplars of English involvement in the new science, and references to the Copernican hypothesis and the support lent it by the observations of Galileo and the calculations of Kepler abound in the works of English baroque authors—Robert Burton, Sir Thomas Browne, George Herbert, the young John Milton, and, very markedly, John Donne.

As for heightened religious concerns, any comparison of representative English texts of the last few decades of the sixteenth century with those of the earlier seventeenth century will reveal the degree to which a hectic religiosity had become one of the hallmarks of the new century. The account of Donne's life given in the first chapter has indicated the extent to which the poet participated in the supercharged and highly partisan religious spirit of his age, and it is worth noting again that even his love poetry is permeated with the language and the concepts of religious experience.

Donne and the Baroque

The longer baroque religious poem expresses a turning away from secular subjects and allegorical modes and their replacement with a direct and nonallegorical engagement of biblical or other overtly religious material. Spenser's typically Renaissance allegorization of romance material in *The Faerie Queene* is replaced by the directly religious epic—Giles Fletcher's *Christ's Victory and Triumph,* Crashaw's *Sospetto d'Herode* (a translation from Marino's Italian poem), Cowley's *Davideis,* and finally, triumphantly, Milton's *Paradise Lost.* Donne did not essay the epic (if one discounts his satiric fragment, *The Progresse of the Soule*), but his longest poetic work, the *Anniversaries,* shows the same urgent, sober, and direct confrontation of the religious issue.

That Donne was deeply aware of the new science and its implications for a Christian world view is a commonplace of literary history. The lines most frequently quoted to exemplify that concern are the following from his "First Anniversarie":

> And new Philosophy calls all in doubt,
> The Element of fire is quite put out;
> The Sun is lost, and th'earth, and no mans wit
> Can well direct him where to looke for it.
> And freely men confesse that this world's spent,
> When in the Planets and the Firmament
> They seeke so many new; they see that this
> Is crumbled out againe to his Atomies.
> 'Tis all in peeces, all cohaerence gone;
> All just supply, and all Relation.[7]

But there are many others as well. In the "Second Anniversarie," for example, Donne presents a vision of the soul's ascent to Heaven:

> Thinke thy shell broke, thinke thy Soule hatch'd but now.
> And think this slow-pac'd soule, which late did cleave
> To'a body, and went but by the bodies leave,
> Twenty, perchance, or thirty mile a day,
> Dispatches in a minute all the way
> Twixt heaven, and earth; she stayes not in the ayre,
> To looke what Meteors there themselves prepare;
> She carries no desire to know, nor sense,
> Whether th'ayres middle region be intense;
> For th'Element of fire, she doth not know,
> Whether she past by such a place or no;
> She baits not at the Moone, nor cares to trie
> Whether in that new world, men live, and die.

(1:256–57)

And near the end of the *Devotions upon Emergent Occasions,* describing his rising from his sickbed, he writes as follows: "I am up, and I seem to stand, and I go round; and I am a new argument of the new philosophy that the earth moves round. Why may I not believe that the whole earth moves in a round motion, though that seem to me to stand, when as I seem to stand to my company, and yet am carried in a giddy and circular motion as I stand?"[8]

Like many of his contemporaries both English and Continental, Donne was neither a champion nor an opponent of the new scientific theories. Apparently he neither believed nor disbelieved but remained in uncertainty, troubled to be sure by some of their implications. The passage from the *Devotions* expresses that uncertainty in a kind of grimly comic tone, and the lines from the "Second Anniversarie" affirm that the truth or falsity of the new science is ultimately irrelevant to the true concern of the soul, which is salvation. The attitude anticipates that of Raphael in *Paradise Lost,* who assures Adam that the nature of the "celestial motions" ought really to be of no concern to him (and Milton, one might note, was a more committed adherent of the Copernican system than Donne ever was). Indeed, Donne's sensitive awareness of the new ideas seem to have had the effect of saturating his poetry and prose with references to the *old* ideas—the Ptolemaic system, the doctrine of universal correspondences, alchemy, the hierarchical vision of the universe—as if such references might constitute a kind of comforting certainty, however much the nervous and experimental quality of his style might demonstrate the opposite.

Baroque and Donne's Literary Style

If the styles of Donne and his contemporaries betray the influence of such extraliterary stimuli as religion and philosophy, they may also be seen as demonstrating the infraliterary phenomenon of reaction against a previously dominant literary style. Even before Donne's earliest writings, signs had appeared in England of a tiring of the literary conventions, especially those governing lyric poetry, that had dominated the European imagination for close to a century (considerably longer in Italy). Sidney professed impatience with Petrarchan conventions, and the Shakespeare of the sonnets sometimes turned them upside down. The devotional lyric—which differs from the religious lyric in general in its more personal quality, its private tone, and its quasi-dramatic organization—had appeared in England before Donne in the works of Robert Southwell and William Alabaster (as, in France, in the works of Sponde and La Ceppède).[9] The genre was to be perfected in England by Donne, and, in the poems of Herbert, Crashaw, and Vaughan, was to become one of the major genres of English poetry in the seventeenth century. What was true of the religious lyric was equally true of the love lyric, occasional poetry, and works in prose, and nowhere is that reaction more obvious than in Donne.

He himself speaks often of his "harshness" or "roughness"; he often violates deliberately the decorum of the Petrarchan tradition; and he parodies Christopher Marlowe's most popular lyric.[10] Many of the features that his critics have most often noted about his poetry—its intellectualized diction, its wide-ranging imagery, its sexual realism, its conceits, its avoidance of sensuous imagery, and its mythological reference[11]—may be taken as symptoms of a conscious revolt. And his prose style constitutes, fully as much, a rebellion against the norms of Renaissance writing. Baroque prose, as seen, for example, in Montaigne, is characterized by a colloquial immediacy and a formal asymmetry, reflecting a consistent impulse to replace the oratorical formality of the Ciceronian style with a kind of period that aspires to give the impression of a mind in the very process of forming its thoughts. What is involved—in the prose of Montaigne, Bacon, Burton, Pascal, or Donne—is not the replacement of art with artlessness but rather the substitution of a different kind of art, one that has affinities with the drama or the meditation rather than with the oration. Almost any passage from Donne's *Sermons* or *Devotions* could be used to illustrate his participation in this baroque movement toward anti-Ciceronian or, as it was sometimes called, Attic prose, but the following passage from *Sermon* XIV of the 1649 folio will serve as well as any:

Ask where that iron is that is ground off a knife or axe; ask that marble that is worn off of the threshold in the church porch by continual treading; and with that iron and with that marble thou mayst find thy father's skin and body; *contrita sunt,* the knife, the marble, the skin, the body are ground away, trod away; they are destroyed. Who knows the revolutions of dust? Dust upon the king's highway and dust upon the king's grave are both, or neither, dust royal and may change places. Who knows the revolutions of dust?[12]

Or this, from the *Devotions upon Emergent Occasions:*

But what have I done, either to *breed* or to *breath* these *vapors?* They tell me
it is my *Melancholy;* did I infuse, did I drinke in *Melancholly* into my self? It
is my *thoughtfulnesse;* was I not made to *thinke?* It is my *study;* doth not my
Calling call for that? I have don nothing wilfully, perversly toward it, yet
must suffer in it, die by it; There are too many *Examples* of men, that have
bin their own *executioners,* and that have made hard shift to be so; some have
alwayes had *poyson* about them, in a *hollow ring* upon their finger, and some
in their *Pen* that they used to write with: some have beat out their *braines* at
the wal of their prison, and some have eate the *fire* out of their
chimneys. . . . But I doe nothing upon my selfe, and yet am mine own
Executioner.[13]

   To summarize, the baroque period in European culture was conditioned in part by innovations in scientific and philosophical thought,
in part by a heightened religious sensibility. The modern reader
should be aware, of course, that these extraliterary influences included
not only thinkers like Galileo, Kepler, Bruno, and Machiavelli,
whose findings have been at least partially validated by subsequent
thought, but also figures who, like Paracelsus, strike us as distant and
quaint. (It is worth noting, for example, that the four great "innovators" who are in Hell in Donne's witty *Ignatius His Conclave* are Galileo, Machiavelli, Paracelsus, and Ignatius of Loyola.) One must also
recognize that the thinkers and artists of the baroque are reacting not
only to intellectual stimuli provided by their own contemporaries but
also to ideas from thinkers of an earlier generation: the earlier seventeenth century is the age of Copernicus in the same sense in which the
later twentieth century is the age of Marx and Freud. It takes time for
intellectual innovation to percolate within a culture.
   But, baroque literary style is also the product of the internal
rhythms of literary history itself. Its stylistic features are to be explained in part as the result of a reaction against literary norms that
appeared to have exhausted themselves. Sometimes the reaction took
the form of extravagant, phantasmagoric ornamentation—the high
baroque; sometimes it took the form of intellectualized, nervous, distorted, and dramatic formulation—the Metaphysical, or mannerist
style. Both options constituted a rejection of the idealistic and mi-
metic tendencies of the Renaissance, and both options, in their wilder
commitment to the activities of the imagination, imply what is perhaps *the* defining feature of the baroque sensibility—a radical and

abiding doubt as to the reality of the phenomenal world. It is that doubt that may explain the baroque fondness for two venerable topoi: the world-as-theater and life-as-a-dream.

Like Shakespeare, like Calderón, Donne, early and late, was obsessed by these topoi. We shall find them turning up frequently as we trace his literary achievement from the juvenilia to the masterpieces of his maturity. Along with other traits of style and habits of vision, they mark Donne as a person of his age even if, like all great artists, he also transcends it.

Chapter Three

Juvenilia, Satyres, Early Elegies

Juvenilia

One item in the Donne canon bears the title *Juvenilia: or Certaine Paradoxes and Problemes:* like most of Donne's poetic works, these prose exercises were first published posthumously, in this case in 1633. There is some uncertainty as to the time of composition: it appears that the *Paradoxes* belong to Donne's early manhood whereas the *Problemes* were written at a somewhat later date.[1] Nevertheless, both types of composition illustrate aspects of the poet's personality—insolence, skepticism, a desire to shock—that were more conspicuously present in his youth than in his mature years. In their form—the intellectualized, quasi-legal, quasi-philosophical defense of outrageous propositions or the witty and cynical presentation of answers to facetious problems—these slight pieces inevitably remind the reader of some of the lyric "evaporations" in the *Songs and Sonets*—such poems as "The Indifferent," "Communitie," and "Confined Love," as well as some of the *Elegies.* They reflect Donne's exposure to a legalistic and rhetorical Renaissance education (some may well have been composed while he was studying at the Inns of Court), and they also indicate something of his sensitivity to the currents of fashionable naturalism and skepticism current in London intellectual circles during the 1590s.

A few titles will indicate the nature of the *Paradoxes and Problemes:* among the *Paradoxes*—"A Defense of Womens Inconstancy," "That Women Ought to Paint," "That a Wise Man is Known by Much Laughing," "That the Gifts of the Body Are Better Than Those of the Minde"; among the *Problemes*—"Why Puritans Make Long Sermons?" "Why Doth the Poxe Soo Much Affect to Undermine the Nose?" "Why Are Courtiers Sooner Atheists Than Men of Other Conditions?" As an example, one might consider the *Probleme* on Puritan sermons, which typifies the brash wit of these pieces as well as the fixed hostility toward the Puritans that was characteristic of the young London intellectuals of the nineties:

It needs not for *perspicuousness,* for God knows they are plain enough: nor do all of them use *Sem-brief-Accents,* for some of them have *Crotchets* [with a pun on *crotchet: quarter-note* and *crotchet: eccentricity,* as opposed to semi-breve: whole note] enough. It may be they intend not to rise like *glorious Tapers* and *Torches,* but like *Thin-wretched-sick-watching-Candles,* which *languish* and are in a Divine *Consumption* from the first minute, yea in their *snuff,* and *stink,* when others are in their more profitable *glory.* I have thought sometimes, that out of conscience, they allow *long measure* to course ware. And sometimes, that *usurping* in that place a *liberty* to *speak freely* of *Kings,* they would *reigne* as long as they could. But now I think they do it out of a *zealous* imagination, that, *It is their duty to Preach on till their Auditory wake.* [2]

Other of Donne's works might qualify as belonging to his juvenilia: the *Epigrams,* the *Satyres,* some of the *Elegies,* and those of the *Verse Letters* that were composed, as indicated by dating, occasion, or reference, during his earliest period of literary creation. Some of the *Songs and Sonets* were surely also written during this earliest period, but it is impossible to date any of them with confidence. *Metempsychosis: The Progresse of the Soule* (1601) is a work transitional between Donne's early manner and the manner of his first mature works.

Although they were highly esteemed by his contemporaries, Donne's epigrams have little that raises them above the general level achieved by Renaissance and baroque practitioners of that classical genre. They play almost no role in modern estimates of the poet's achievement. Still, some of them are very funny, as, for example, this epigram on an "Antiquary": "If in his Studie he hath so much care / To 'hang all old strange things, let his wife beware" (1:77). His satires are of an altogether different order of importance, ranking among the most important of his earlier works. Religion is an important theme in these poems—in *Satyre* III, the question of which Christian church possessed the truth; in *Satyres* II and IV, the persecution of the English Catholics. The figure of the "pursevant," or informer against suspected Catholics, is one important object of satire, and others include such familiar targets as courtiers, fops, poetasters, lawyers, and nouveaux riches.

Satyres

The genre of formal verse satire enjoyed striking popularity in the England of the 1590s, but the reader whose conceptions of the form have been shaped by the work of such later satirists as Dryden and

Pope will be puzzled by many aspects of the satiric poems of Donne, John Marston, Joseph Hall, and others of the period. For them, satire was conceived as a genre that was general in its abuse, deliberately rough in its meter, cacophonous in its diction, and obscure in its reference. In consequence, their practice contrasts strongly with that of Dryden and Pope—personal in its targets, lucid in both meaning and construction, and viciously polished in style. The following lines from Donne's *Satyre* II may serve to exemplify some of the features of the Elizabethan genre:

> When sicke with Poëtrie, and possest with muse
> Thou wast, and mad, I hop'd; but men which chuse
> Law practise for meere gaine, bold soule, repute
> Worse than imbrothel'd strumpets prostitute.
> Now like an owelike watchman, hee must walke
> His hand still at a bill, now he must talke
> Idly, like prisoners, which whole months will sweare
> That only suretiship hath brought them there,
> And to every suitor lye in every thing,
> Like a Kings favourite, yea like a King.
>   (1:152)

The willful ruggedness of Elizabethan satire may be traced to a false etymology current at the time: believing that the word *satire* derives from *satyr* (rather than, as is the case, from the Latin *satura*, [medley]), the poets devised a style that they felt might appropriately proceed from a savage, uncivilized, hairy wood-creature.[3] Committed still to the practice of the imitation of the ancients, Donne and his fellows took the Roman satirists Juvenal and, especially, Persius as their models, eschewing the manner of the more urbane and less savage Horace. The vogue of formal satire in Elizabethan England was short-lived. In 1599 the Court of High Commission, concerned over possible expressions of political dissent, prohibited the further printing of satires without specific permission. The satiric spirit migrated to the theater of Jonson and Shakespeare.

In *Satyre* I Donne vents the speaker's contempt and annoyance at a stupid, superficial, and would-be-fashionable fop who has accosted him on the street; *Satyre* II deals with a bad poet who has become a bad lawyer; *Satyre* III handles the question of religious truth and the difficulties in searching for it; *Satyre* IV presents the experience of the speaker with an informer who is trying to trick him into saying something that may be construed as sympathy with the Catholic cause; and *Satyre* V attacks both the venal persons who bring legal suits and the corrupt officials who fleece them. Of the *Satyres,* III, with intense evocation of the necessary religious quest and the psychological obstacles to it, is surely the most powerful and dramatic, as well as being the one in which wit is used most purposefully—rather than, as so often in the young Donne, for its own sake alone.

Metempsychosis: The Progresse of the Soule (1601), referred to briefly in Chapter 1, is subtitled "Poema Satyricon" and may well be considered here. The governing doctrine of this extravagant work is that of the transmigration of souls, and the poet wittily undertakes to recount the adventures and transformations of the soul of heresy beginning with its first lodging place in the apple eaten by Adam and Eve. Subsequent hosts include a mandrake, a sparrow, a fish, a swan, a whale, a mouse, a wolf, and an ape, after which the poem breaks off. Ben Jonson told Drummond of Hawthornden that Donne had intended to make the soul's last resting place the person of John Calvin,[4] but most critics believe that the fragment implies that the soul of heresy is to be finally incarnated in none other than Donne's own monarch, Queen Elizabeth.

The satiric nature of this fragment is obvious, but in form, tone, and technique it is very different from the verse satires of the 1590s. Among other things it is a narrative poem and, as such, gives the reader some sense of what the poet might have accomplished, had he chosen to work more in narrative genres. Furthermore it is composed not in couplets but in a curious stanza form, which seems to owe something to Spenser (Donne's great opposite in so many respects): the stanza consists of ten lines rhyming *aabccbbddd,* all lines iambic pentameter except for the tenth, which is hexameter. It makes far more use of sensuous and descriptive imagery than is usually the case with Donne, a fact worth noting in view of the often-urged contention that Donne's poetry is virtually devoid of sensuous qualities: it seems possible that the relative significance given to sensuous imagery in Donne's work is related to the various genres in which he worked, and to his sense of the different decorums indicated for those genres.

The following stanza, describing the ape's attempted seduction of one of Eve's daughters, will give some sense of the poem as a whole:

> First she was silly and knew not what he meant.
> That vertue, by his touches, chaft and spent,

Succeeds an itchie warmth, that melts her quite;
She knew not first, nowe cares not what he doth,
And willing halfe and more, more than halfe loth,
She neither puls nor pushes, but outright
Now cries, and now repents; when *Tethlemite*
Her brother, enterd, and a great stone threw
After the Ape, who, thus prevented, flew.
   This house thus batter'd downe, the Soule possest a new.
                                                                   (1:314)

And the last stanza of the fragment, with its Hamlet-like concluding lines, typifies the skepticism and intellectuality not of the young
Donne alone but also of England and Europe at the dawn of the seventeenth century:

Who ere thou beest that read'st this sullen Writ,
Which just so much courts thee, as thou dost it,
Let me arrest thy thoughts; wonder with mee,
Why plowing, building, ruling and the rest
Or most of those arts, whence our lives are blest,
By cursed *Caines* race invented be,
And blest *Seth* vext us with Astronomie,
Ther's nothing simply good, nor ill alone,
Of every quality comparison,
   The onely measure is, and judge, opinion.
                                                                   (1:315–16)

Donne and Wit

Donne's early works—indeed all his works—are dominated by the
quality the seventeenth century called *wit*. That English word has a
complex and interesting history. From Anglo-Saxon times until the
Age of Elizabeth it meant simply *intelligence*—a meaning that survives
in such modern terms and phrases as *half-wit* or *at my wit's end*. More
generally, however, in modern English the term *wit* has developed a
more restricted meaning, as "quickness of mental activity, capacity
for intellectual and verbal humor, ability to make wise-cracks." From
the late sixteenth/early seventeenth century until well into the eighteenth, the meaning of the term lies somewhere in between its original
and its modern meanings, and it is in that sense that Donne's contemporaries ascribed to the poet a superlative degree of wit, so that
he had the reputation of being the greatest "wit" of his day.

In baroque psychology, the two mental capacities deemed most important for poetic creation were *judgment* and *wit* (with *fancy* as a popular competing synonym for the latter). *Judgment* meant the ability to see the differences between apparently similar phenomena; *wit* or *fancy,* the ability to see the similarities between apparently different phenomena.[5] Wit is thus the basis for the favorite baroque poetic device, the conceit, or extravagant metaphor—a device so highly favored as to be virtually a definition of baroque poetic style.

Thomas Hobbes, in his "Answer to Davenant's Preface before *Gondibert*" (1650), tells us in a famous passage that "Judgement begets the strength and structure, and Fancy begets the ornaments of a Poem."[6] But Hobbes is in many respects, despite the dates of his long life, a precursor of neoclassicism; for many more typically baroque literary figures, both in England and on the Continent, fancy, or wit (Italian *ingegno,* Spanish *ingenio,* French *esprit*), is the primary source of strength and structure as well as of ornament. It was, to the baroque mind, a sufficient criterion for poetry, as qualities such as sensous imagination and apparent emotional sincerity were to become sufficient criteria in the romantic era.

Although theories of wit or *ingegno/ingenio* did not play as significant a role in the expressed thought of seventeenth-century English critics as they did in that of their Italian or Spanish contemporaries, the poetic practice of Donne and the other Metaphysicals clearly reveals the importance of the concept. In Donne's *Satyres* and his *Metempsychosis,* wit is at the service of poetic motives beyond itself, as, in his *Songs and Sonets* and many of his *Elegies,* it is in the service of erotic or amorous themes. But in most of his early *Verse Letters,* as in the *Paradoxes and Problemes,* wit is the very raison d'être of the poem.

Donne's *Verse Letters*

Donne's *Verse Letters,* for most modern readers the most inaccessible of his poetic works, fall into two fairly well-defined groups.[7] The first is made up of epistles written to friends of the poet's youth—Christopher Brooke, Rowland Woodward, Thomas Woodward, and Sir Henry Wotton (these poems are to be dated ca. 1597–1608). The second group, to be considered in a later chapter, consists mostly of ingenious poems of compliment addressed to the great ladies who were, during the period of Donne's poverty, at once his patronesses and the recipients of his Platonic devotion. Among the early verse letters are

"The Storme" and "The Calme," products of the poet's participation
in the expedition of Essex against the Azores in 1597. Greatly admired by Ben Jonson, these are companion pieces—examples of a
genre dear to the hearts of baroque poets and exemplified most fa-
mously by Milton's "L'Allegro" and "Il Penseroso." In theme, both
poems are almost ridiculously simple: they tell the reader (nominally
Christopher Brooke) how stormy the storm was, and how calm the
calm. Donne's whole purpose is to demonstrate the extravagance of
his wit in enunciating those simple themes. The following lines, from
"The Calme," are typical:

> As steady 'as I can wish, that my thoughts were,
> Smooth as thy mistresse glasse, or what shines there,
> The sea is now. And, as the Iles which wee
> Seeke, when wee can move, our ships rooted bee.
> As water did in stormes, now pitch runs out:
> As lead, when a fir'd Church becomes one spout.
> And all our beauty, and our trimme, decayes,
> Like courts removing, or like ended playes.
> The fighting place now seamens ragges supply;
> And all the tackling is a frippery.
> No use of lanthornes; and in one place lay
> Feathers and dust, to day and yesterday.
>
> (1:178)

The epistles to Wotton (himself a gifted poet and an important
diplomat) are thematically more substantial: the one beginning "Sir,
more than kisses, letters mingle Soules" comments on the vices native
to the court, the country, and the city (the three traditional sociologi-
cal categories of Renaissance and baroque thought), and recommends
an ethos of individual and rather stoical self-reliance; similar attitudes
inform the one beginning "Went you to conquer."

Donne's three epithalamia, or wedding poems, belong in tone and
manner with the *Verse Letters*. The earliest, the "Epithalamion Made
at Lincolnes Inne," dates from his student years and, though witty,
displays qualities of sensuous imagination appropriate to the genre, if
atypical of the poet.

Early Elegies

Donne's twenty *Elegies*, like his *Verse Letters*, may be divided into
two groups. The first, and larger, belongs to the 1590s and consists

of love poems, most of them, as previously noted, modeled on Ovid's *Amores*. The second group, *Elegie* IX, and *Elegies* XII through XX, either belong to the period 1600 and later or are spurious (Gardner doubts the authorship of XII, XIII, XIV, XV, XVII—the numbers cited are the traditional ones employed in the Grierson edition);[8] their subject matter is varied, and they will be dealt with in a later section of this study.

The early *Elegies* sparkle with extravagant wit, but, in contrast to most of the *Verse Letters,* the wit is pressed into the service of dramatic and psychological motives. In the manner of the *Songs and Sonets,* most of the love elegies have the form of an immediate and conversational address to an implied interlocutor. In *Elegie* I the speaker expostulates with his mistress, a married woman who is distressed by the manifestations of her husband's jealousy:

> Fond woman, which would'st have thy husband die,
> And yet complain'st of his great jealousy;
> If swolne with poyson, hee lay in'his last bed,
> His body with a sere-barke covered. . .
> Thou would'st not weepe, but jolly, 'and frolicke bee,
> As a slave, which to morrow should be free;
> Yet weep'st thou, when thou seest him hungerly
> Swallow his owne death, hearts-bane jealousie.
>
> (1:79)

The dominant tone is impatience—with the husband, who is hated not so much because of the lover's passion for the woman as because he constitutes an inconvenience, and with the mistress, whose sensitivity presents a kind of roadblock to his importunate lust. The poem concludes with the suggestion that the lovers find another location for their trysts:

> There we will scorne his houshold policies,
> His seely plots, and pensionary spies,
> As the inhabitants of Thames right side
> Do Londons Major [i.e., "mayor"]; or Germans, the Popes pride.
>
> (1:80)

(Southwark, on the right bank of the Thames, was technically not a part of the city of London, and hence not subject to the authority of the Lord Mayor of London, who, representing the dominantly puritanical citizenry, banned many pleasures, including the theater.)

The speaker in *Elegie* IV is comparably self-centered, cynical, materialistic, and even brutal, but the situation is different and the wit is more exuberant and high-spirited. In IV, subtitled "The Perfume," the obstacle to the fulfillment of the lovers' lust is not a husband but a father—as implacably hostile to the speaker as Sir George More, in real life, was to Donne. The poet spares no pains to express detestation for the father, the mother, and the entire household that stands between him and his pleasure. Conceit and hyperbole are his principal weapons, and the following lines, an invective against the domestic who serves as a kind of household sentry, well exemplify the poet's skill with those weapons:

> The grim eight-foot-high iron-bound serving-man,
> That oft names God in oathes, and onely then,
> He that to barre the first gate, doth as wide
> As the great Rhodian Colossus stride,
> Which, if in hell no other paines there were,
> Makes mee feare hell, because he must be there:
> Though by thy father he were hir'd to this,
> Could never witnesse any touch or kisse.
>   (1:85)

The subject of the poem is the perfume with which the speaker has sneaked into the house of his beloved. Presumably a gift for her, the perfume has spilled, and its fragrance reveals his presence to his enemies. The apostrophe to the traitorous perfume demonstrates a capacity for inventive denunciation that rivals that of an ancient Celtic curse:

> Base excrement of earth, which dost confound
> Sense, from distinguishing the sicke from sound;
> By thee the seely Amorous sucks his death
> By drawing in a leprous harlots breath;
> By thee, the greatest staine to mans estate
> Falls on us, to be call'd effeminate;
> Though you be much lov'd in the Princes hall,
> There, things that seeme, exceed substantiall.
> Gods, when yee fum'd on altars, were pleas'd well,
> Because you'were burnt, not that they lik'd your smell.
>   (I:85–86)

The last of the quoted couplets incorporates a device typical of Metaphysical wit at its most radical. One might call it the "willful misprision," in which the poem feigns to understand a phenomenon in terms clearly opposed to those in which it is obviously meant to be understood (another example may be found, two generations later, in Andrew Marvell's "The Garden": "Apollo hunted Daphne so / Only that she might laurel grow, / And Pan did after Syrinx speed / Not as a Nymph, but for a reed").[9] Donne is fond of the device.

Elegie VII is similar in tone and attitude to I and IV, but the dramatic situation is significantly different in that the obstacle to the speaker's lust is not a husband or father but rather the partner herself. As the poem tells us, the speaker, a kind of Pygmalion of lasciviousness, has educated his mistress in the arcane mysteries of a love affair. She has profited from the education to such a degree that she has declared independence from her tutor and taken another lover. The speaker's righteous indignation and sense of injured merit know no bounds, as he reproaches her. It might be illuminating to quote in full this masterful example of Donne's dramatic method:

> Natures lay Ideòt, I taught thee to love,
> And in that sophistrie, Oh, thou dost prove
> Too subtile: Foole, thou didst not understand
> The mystic language of the eye nor hand:
> Nor couldst thou judge the difference of the aire
> Of sighes, and say, this lies, this sounds despaire:
> Nor by the'eyes water call a maladie
> Desperately hot, or changing feaverously.
> I had not taught thee then, the Alphabet
> Of flowers, how they devisefully being set
> And bound up, might with speechlesse secrecie
> Deliver arrands mutely, and mutually.
> Remember since all thy words us'd to bee
> To every suitor; I [i.e., aye] *if my friends agree;*
> Since, household charmes, thy husbands name to teach
> Were all the love trickes, that thy wit could reach;
> And since, an houres discourse could scarce have made
> One answer in thee, and that ill arraid
> In broken proverbs, and torne sentences.
> Thou art not by so many duties his,
> That from the worlds Common having sever'd thee,
> Inlaid thee, neither to be seene, nor see,
> As mine: who have with amorous delicacies
> Refin'd thee'into a blis-ful Paradise.
> Thy graces and good words my creatures bee;
> I planted knowledge and lifes tree in thee,

Which Oh, shall strangers taste? Must I alas
Frame and enamell Plate, and drinke in Glasse?
Chafe waxe for others seales? breake a colts force
And leave him then, beeing made a ready horse?

                                                                     (1:90)

Lines 15–16 may be puzzling. The allusion is to girlish superstitions
having to do with spells to determine the identity of one's future husband (cf. Keats's Madeline in "The Eve of St. Agnes").

Many features of *Elegie* VII parallel the obsessions of the *Songs and
Sonets:* the conception of love as an arcane mystery like medicine or,
even more, religion—something that sets its practitioners apart from
the *profanum vulgus;* the desire for absolute possession of the beloved;
the insistence on the physicality of love. The gross sexuality of the
concluding images (e.g., "lifes tree," "ready horse") is reinforced by
the fact that, in the English of Donne's time, the word "seals" carried
the colloquial meaning "sexual organs."

Not all of Donne's love elegies are as dramatic and psychological as
I, IV, and VII. *Elegie* II, "The Anagram," is a flippantly witty description of an ugly woman, a parody of the *blason* of female beauty
so dear to the love poets of the High Renaissance. *Elegie* III,
"Change," is a poem in praise of variety and inconstancy, a recurrent
minor theme of the *Songs and Sonets.* In *Elegie* V, "The Picture," the
speaker gives his beloved a picture of himself before he departs for the
wars: it is thus probably more strongly autobiographical than most of
the *Elegies.* And *Elegie* VIII, "The Comparison," is another extravagant evocation of female ugliness.

Helen Gardner believes that *Elegie* X, "The Dreame," ought to be
classified with the *Songs and Sonets* rather than with the *Elegies.*[10] The
fact of its occurrence as an "elegie" in some of the manuscript collections argues further the thematic connections between these two
classes of poems. Despite the dramatic—and often dramatized—nature of many of the *Elegies,* few readers would doubt that there is an
ultimate link between their content and the personal experience of the
poet. They are unlikely to have been written by a celibate, or even
by a person of rather limited sexual experience. The same is true of
the *Songs and Sonets,* to which we now turn. It is on these poems,
together with the *Holy Sonnets* and the *Hymnes,* that John Donne's
modern reputation as a poet chiefly rests.

Chapter Four
Songs and Sonets

Donne's love lyrics were not published during his lifetime but circulated only in manuscript collections, a fact that accounts for the notorious difficulty of dating any of them. In the first, posthumous edition of his poems (1633), they appeared scattered at random throughout the volume, but in the next edition (1635) they were grouped together under the title *Songs and Sonets*. Both that designation and the order in which the second edition presented the poems have generally been retained in subsequent editions. That order is capricious and without authority, chronological or other, but, probably by chance, the first six poems are virtually definitive examples of the three classes into which Donne's love poems fall: exalted and idealistic expressions of a constant love ("The Good-Morrow," "The Sunne Rising"), lightly cynical "evaporations" ("Goe, and catch a falling starre," "Womans Constancy," "The Indifferent"), and protestations of a rather conventionally Platonic nature ("The Undertaking").

General Characteristics

Inevitably, many of Donne's critics have found in the inconsistency and mutual incompatibility of Donne's amorous attitudes a possible guide to the chronology of the poems. Reading them as straightforward autobiographical documents, scholars have posited that the evaporations are early, expressing the attitudes of young Jack Donne the rake, whereas the more idealistic poems and the Platonic poems are later works, composed after Donne had been reformed by the love of a good woman (Ann More, of course). Apart from the unprovability of such assumptions and apart, too, from the fact that they betray a continuing reliance on Walton's unreliable account, they posit a modern, or at least a postromantic, conception of lyric creation—that the lyric is a direct and sincere expression of the poet's own experience. A consideration of Donne's work as a whole ought to suggest the degree to which he shared with other baroque poets a conception

of the lyric as dramatic, fictive, and in the seventeenth-century sense
of that term, "artificial."

This is not to say, of course, that there is *no* connection between
the *Songs and Sonets* and the personal emotional experience of their author. On the contrary, the man who wrote the poems had experienced
much, lusted mightily, and loved deeply. But while the poems derive
from personal experience, they do not document it. Taken as a whole,
the *Songs and Sonets* remind us, with a power matched by few collections of love lyrics, just what a complicated, contradictory, mysteri-
ous, and overwhelming matter sexual love is. The same human being
can—in different moods rather than at different stages of life—be ra-
pacious or desperately tender, exalt the spirit or the flesh, revel in
sexual variety or seek with unbearable longing a love that is absolute
in its constancy. All this, and much more, is to be found in the *Songs
and Sonets,* and that richness is one of the qualities that make Donne,
arguably, the greatest love poet in English literature.[1]

One may as well begin with "The Good-Morrow":

> I wonder by my troth, what thou, and I
> Did, till we lov'd? were we not wean'd till then?
> But suck'd on countrey pleasures, childishly?
> Or snorted we in the seaven sleepers den?
> T'was so; But this, all pleasures fancies bee.
> If ever any beauty I did see,
> Which I desir'd, and got, t'was but a dreame of thee.
>
>   (1:7)

The departures from the norms of Renaissance poetry are radical and
striking. Whereas Sidney, Spenser, and their Continental contemporaries had typically written a kind of quasi-public poetry, in which
some third party (the reader, in most cases) is told *about* the beloved,
her beauty, virtue, cruelty, unattainability, or whatever, Donne addresses the beloved directly—the reader is placed in the position not
of audience but of eavesdropper. The Renaissance poets had, furthermore, almost always followed their master Petrarch in making of the
beloved a distant goddess figure, infinitely desired but infinitely unat-
tainable; Donne celebrates a consummated love, addressing his mistress in a situation of great intimacy after a night of love.

In other respects as well the baroque poet contrasts with his Renaissance predecessors. Renaissance love poetry never tires of evoking
the physical beauty of the beloved, detailing her manifold charms

with great sensuous vividness and with the expenditure of a whole arsenal of decorous images derived from flowers, celestial orbs, precious stones, and precious metals, as well as allusions to Greco-Roman mythology. Donne makes no effort to evoke the appearance of his beloved; the reader will search in vain, in *Songs and Sonets,* for any indication of the color of his love's hair or eyes, or the specific nature of her softness and sweetness. And the poet eschews the conventional images of description for a range of metaphors embracing such diverse areas of activity as astronomy, cartography, nautical exploration, geometry, and philosophy. Spenser and his fellows had cultivated and perfected smooth and regular metrics, combined with other auditory devices in a virtuoso manner to produce a quasi-musical effect. Donne, in contrast, deploys metrical irregularities and discords in such a way as to achieve a mimesis of passionate conversation. Consider, for example, the remarkably different effects of a typical opening of one of Spenser's *Amoretti* and the beginning of "The Good-Morrow":

> What guyle is this, that these her golden tresses
> She doth disguise under a net of gold.[2]

and

> I wonder by my troth, what thou, and I
> Did, till we lov'd? were we not wean'd till then?

Of equal importance, and of equal novelty in the tradition of English love poetry, is Donne's concern with the psychological. The stanza quoted from "The Good-Morrow" might, on a superficial reading, be taken as memorializing the discovery of sexual love by a young man and woman who have just lost their virginity. A more careful reading will demonstrate—as Clay Hunt and others have pointed out—something quite different.[3] The word "pleasures" in line 5 carries a distinct sexual connotation; "countrey"—used as an adjective in line 3—has comparable implications (cf. Hamlet to Ophelia: "Do you think I meant country matters? [act 3, scene 2, line 123]); and, in this context, the word "beauty" (1.6) seems not abstract but concrete—a reference to "belles" the speaker has previously "got." It is *spiritual* love that the lovers have found—but spirit cannot be severed from flesh, as the second stanza makes clear:

And now good morrow to our waking soules,
Which watch not one another out of feare;
For love, all love of other sights controules,
And makes one little roome, an every where.
Let sea-discoverers to new worlds have gone,
Let Maps to other, worlds on worlds have shown,
Let us possess one world, each hath one, and is one.
(1:7)

The third and final stanza concludes the poem with the logical rigor characteristic of all Donne's lyrics, and it also demonstrates, all but definitively, the fondness for conceit and for intellectual reference that serves, virtually, as a definition of Metaphysical poetry:

My face in thine eye, thine in mine appeares,
And true plaine hearts doe in the faces rest,
Where can we finde two better hemispheres
Without sharp North, without declining West?
What ever dyes, was not mixt equally;
If our two loves be one, or, thou and I
Love so alike, that none doe slacken, none can die.
(1:7–8)

The ingenious image that opens the stanza is a reference to the universal and quite charming lovers' custom of gazing deep into each other's eyes—a custom that sixteenth-and seventeenth-century English called "looking babies" (Donne employs it also in "The Extasie")—but it undergoes extraordinary development at Donne's hands. Each lover, gazing into the partner's eyes, sees his/her face reflected, but at the same time sees the lover's eyeball as a hemisphere. Two hemispheres joined—and there are two lovers involved—constitute a sphere and thus a world, as well as the traditional symbol of perfection.[4] Donne's obsessive motif of the two lovers' constituting their own world, separate from that of the "laiety," receives powerful articulation.

For a moment, in the next line, the poet modulates uncharacteristically into mythic reference, evoking a perfect world from which the north (bitterness and pain) and the west (death) have been banished. He concludes with an appeal to Aristotelian philosophy, which had held that a substance composed of a perfectly balanced mixture of the four elements (earth, water, air, and fire) is not subject to change or decay. Such passages as this provided the occasion for the epithet *metaphysical,* first applied to Donne's lyrics by Dryden and later expanded by Dr. Johnson to form a concept that established itself as definitive in English (and, latterly, general European) literary historiography.[5]

Such poems as "The Sunne Rising" reiterate the concerns of "The Good-Morrow," though with a different strategy of address. In this poem, rather than addressing the beloved, the speaker apostrophizes the sun—in terms that are scantly respectful in view of the traditional symbolic system of the Renaissance, in which the sun, as the principal planet, corresponds in the astronomical dimension to the head in the anatomical, to the king in the political, to the lion in the animal, to the oak in the vegetable, and to God in totality:

> Busie old foole, unruly Sunne,
> Why dost Thou thus,
> Through windowes, and through curtaines call on us?
> Must to thy motions lovers seasons run?
>
> (1:1–4)

The concluding stanza is notable for the boldness of its hyperbole in elevating the lovers above everything in the world:

> She's all States, and all Princes, I,
> Nothing else is.
> Princes doe but play us; compared to this,
> All honor's mimique; All wealth alchimie.
> Thou sunne art halfe as happy'as wee,
> In that the world's contracted thus;
> Thine age askes ease, and since thy duties bee
> To warme the world, that's done in warming us.
> Shine here to us, and thou art every where;
> This bed thy center is, these walls, thy sphaere.
>
> (1:11–12)

Donne's poems of elevated love assume, with the Platonic tradition, that love is above all spiritual, and that the important aspect of the lovers' union is the joining of their spirits (this idea is examined in great detail in "The Extasie"). But Donne departs from the orthodoxies of Renaissance Neoplatonism by refusing to accept the idea that a perfected love rises above the body and leaves it behind as that

love becomes purely spiritual. If one remembers the popular Neoplatonic image of the ladder of love, in which the lower rungs denote
the purely physical aspects of love, the higher rungs the purely spiritual, one must picture Donne as scampering unabashedly up and
down the ladder. Thus "The Sunne Rising" ends appropriately with
a reference to the bed where human love, spiritual as well as physical,
is consummated.

The Cynical Poems

The value system of the poet's "evaporations" is utterly different,
as a consideration of a typical one, "Womans Constancy," will demonstrate:

> Now thou hast lov'd me one whole day,
> To morrow when thou leav'est, what wilt thou say?
> Wilt thou then Antedate some new made vow?
>   Or say that now
> We are not just those persons, which we were?
> Or, that oathes made in reverentiall feare
> Of Love, and his wrath, any may forsweare?
> Or, as true deaths, true maryages untie,
> So lovers contracts, images of those,
> Binde but till sleep, deaths image, them unloose?
>   Or, your owne end to Justifie,
> For having purpos'd change, and falsehood; you
> Can have no way but falsehood to be true?
> Vaine lunatique, against these scapes I could
> Dispute, and conquer, if I would,
> Which I abstaine to doe,
> For by to morrow, I may thinke so too.

                                                        (1:9)

Arnold Stein has commented perceptively on the nature of the wit in
this and similar poems, in which a series of propositions, each more
outrageously ingenious than the one before it, seems to be leading
in one logical direction, only to be overthrown by an opposed—and
unexpected—proposition yet more outrageously ingenious.[6]
Despite the differences in implied value systems, the exalted poems
and the outrageous ones are nevertheless the products of the same personality and the same imagination. The rationalizations attributed to

the woman being addressed have the same kind of intricacy as the
assertions in "The Good-Morrow"; the argument that oaths made in
fear of love's power are invalid, since they have been forced, reveals
the student of law; the double analogy between marriage vows and
lovers' vows, death and sleep, has the perverse glitter that is one of
Donne's distinguishing features; and the suggestion that she will ar-
gue that a previous intention to be false makes falsehood her only way
of being true shows the poet's love of paradox. The colloquial and
dramatic traits of the poem are also consistent with his entire lyric
work.

The obsessions betrayed by this light piece are also identical with
those found in more serious works. The perception (11. 4–5) that every human being changes—not only mentally but even in actual
physical composition—undergoes tremendous and deeply moving
elaboration in one of Donne's longest and most ambitious works—the
"Second Anniversarie" of 1612—in a passage dwelling on the impossibility of finding a constant love this side of Heaven:

> Dost thou love
> Beauty? (And Beauty worthyest is to move)
> Poore cous'ned cose'nor, that she, and that thou,
> Which did begin to love, are neither now.
> You are both fluid, chang'd since yesterday;
> Next day repaires, (but ill) last daies decay.
> Nor are, (Although the river keep the name)
> Yesterdaies waters, and to daies the same.
> So flowes her face, and thine eies, neither now
> That saint, nor Pilgrime, which your loving vow
> Concernd, remaines; but whil'st you thinke you bee
> Constant, you'are howrely in inconstancee.
>
> (1:262)

"The Flea" is probably the most celebrated of Donne's evaporations—in our day as in his. With exuberant wit the poet argues that
the flea, having sucked blood from both the speaker and the lady, has
mingled their bloods and thus effected already the sexual union that
he desires:

> This flea is you and I, and this
> Our mariage bed, and mariage temple is;

> Though parents grudge, and you, w'are met,
> And cloysterd in these living walls of Jet.
> Though use make you apt to kill mee,
> Let not to that, selfe murder added bee,
> And sacrilege, three sinnes in killing three.
>   (1:40–41)

The wit has been often, and justly, admired, but the dramatic immediacy of the poem is scarcely less admirable. The opening of each of
the poem's three stanzas evokes a situation and a gesture: "Marke but
this flea, and marke in this, / How little that which thou deny'st me
is," "Oh stay, three lives in one flea spare, / Where wee almost, yea
more than maryed are," "Cruell and sodaine, hast thou since /
Purpled thy naile, in blood of innocence." In the first opening, the
speaker draws the woman's attention to a flea crawling on her person;
in the second, with a gesture of his hand, he beseeches her to refrain
from killing the flea; in the third, with a tone of mock distress, he
laments the squashing of the insect. In the interval between each
stanza, the lady performs an action—the attempt to squash the flea
between stanzas 1 and 2, the successful execution of that design between 2 and 3. If it is not too fanciful, the reader may even imagine
the actions of this mute interlocutor, and even her expression. I imagine it as an expression of amused flirtatiousness.

Neoplatonic Poems

Earlier I maintained that Donne the love poet refuses to admit the
conventional Neoplatonic notion of true love's being susceptible to a
refinement that enables it to leave the love of the body behind. Certain of the *Songs and Sonets*—"The Undertaking," "The Blossome,"
"The Relique," and perhaps a couple of others—would seem to call
that contention into question. In "The Undertaking," for example,
the poet writes:

> But he who lovelinesse within
>   Hath found, all outward loathes,
> For he who colour loves, and skinne,
>   Loves but their oldest clothes.
>
> If, as I have, you also doe
>   Vertue'attir'd in woman see,

And dare love that, and say so too,
And forget the Hee and Shee.
(1:10)

And in "The Relique," more circumstantially:

First, we lov'd well and faithfully,
Yet knew not what wee lov'd, nor why,
Difference of sex no more wee knew,
Than our Guardian Angells doe;
Coming and going, we
Perchance might kisse, but not between those meales;
Our hands ne'r toucht the seales,
Which nature, injur'd by late law, sets free.
(1:63)

One must acknowledge the contradiction between such poems and the majority of the *Songs and Sonets,* noting, however, that poems of orthodox Platonism are a distinct minority of the total poems, and remarking also that the poet himself seems sometimes wryly amused by the implications of the orthodox doctrine—as in the conclusion of "The Blossome" (the speaker is addressing his own heart):

Meet mee at London, then,
Twenty dayes hence, and thou shalt see
Mee fresher, and more fat, by being with men,
Than if I had staid still with her and thee.
For Gods sake, if you can, be you so too:
I would give you
There, to another friend, whom wee shall finde
As glad to have my body, as my minde.
(1:60)

It is tempting—although, of course, unprovable—to assume that the poems of conventional Neoplatonism are addressed to Donne's patronesses—the great ladies whom he, during his years of penury, flattered, cajoled, flirted with, sponged off, and perhaps—sometimes, and in some ways—loved (as he may have loved Magdalen Herbert). But all this is conjecture.

Poems of Idealism

More typical, and more numerous, are the lyrics of an exalted love
that will not deny the body, that indeed celebrates it. And in those
poems Donne displays the complexity and variety of the emotion of
sexual love to a degree probably unmatched in any other poetry in
English. Some of those poems are built upon the confusion of physical
love and religious devotion already noted. Such a poem is "The Canonization":

> For Godsake hold your tongue, and let me love,
>   Or chide my palsie, or my gout,
> My five gray haires, or ruin'd fortune flout,
>   With wealth your state, your minde with Arts improve,
>   Take you a course, get you a place,
>   Observe his honour, or his grace,
>   Or the Kings reall, or his stamped face
>   Contemplate, what you will, approve,
>   So you will let me love.
>
>   (1:14)

Like most of Donne's lyrics, this one is dramatic, but here the implied interlocutor is not the beloved but rather a friend or acquaint-
ance, perhaps a young man of his own age. That interlocutor has just
suggested that the speaker's amorous commitment to a certain woman
is excessive, impractical, unwise: we, the readers, eavesdrop on the
response. The stanza that follows is a kind of tour de force, at once
a parody and a modest reaffirmation of the norms of Petrarchan love
poetry:

> Alas, alas, who's injur'd by my love?
>   What merchants ships have my sighs drown'd?
> Who saies my teares have overflow'd his ground?
>   When did my colds a forward spring remove?
>   When did the heats which my veines fill
>   Adde one more to the plaguie Bill?
>   Soldiers finde warres, and Lawyers find out still
>   Litigious men, which quarrels move,
>   Though she and I do love.
>
>   (1:14)

This affirmation is achieved by the simple but brilliant task of inflating the hyperbole to the point of absurdity, simultaneously denying its literal truth and thus maintaining the validity of the emotions it asserts.

The next stanza stresses the adamant physicality of the love relationship by deploying the image of the fly, traditionally associated with lust, and the taper, phallic in implication, with, in addition, the familiar sixteenth-and seventeenth-century pun on "die" as meaning "to experience sexual climax." The union of the lovers is figured by the phoenix:

> Call us what you will, wee are made such by love;
>> Call her one, mee another flye,
> We'are Tapers too, and at our owne cost die,
>> And wee in us finde the'Eagle and the Dove.
>> The Phoenix ridle hath more wit
>> By us, we two being one, are it.
> So to one neutrall thing both sexes fit,
>> Wee dye and rise the same, and prove
>> Mysterious by this love.
>
>> (1:15)

Stanza 4 continues to play with the double meaning of "to die," and it is in that context that the speaker asserts that their exemplary love will cause them to be canonized—like Catholic saints—by the lovers of the future. Those lovers, it is prophesied, will invoke them in the following terms:

> You whom reverend love
> Made one anothers hermitage;
> You, to whom love was peace, that now is rage;
>> Who did the whole worlds soule contract, and drove
>> Into the glasses of your eyes
>> (So made such mirrors, and such spies,
> That they did all to you epitomize,)
>> Countries, Townes, Courts: Beg from above
>> A patterne of your love!
>
>> (1:15)

"The Canonization" contends that the emotion shared by the lovers is in some sense equatable with religious experience. It does not tell

us in quite what sense. Other lyrics, however, investigate the connection more circumstantially; a particularly subtle example is "Lovers
Infinitenesse":

> If yet I have not all thy love,
> Deare, I shall never have it all,
> I cannot breath one other sigh, to move,
> Nor can intreat one other teare to fall,
> And all my treasure, which should purchase thee,
> Sighs, teares, and oathes, and letters I have spent.
> Yet no more can be due to mee,
> Than at the bargaine made was ment,
> If then thy gift of love were partiall,
> That some to mee, some should to others fall,
>   Deare, I shall never have Thee All.
>   (1:17)

Utilizing a range of mundane imagery alien to the decorum of the
Elizabethans, Donne enforces concentration on the intellectual process
of which the stanza is composed. The imagery, commercial and legal,
indicates that the true love he desires is something that can be pur-
chased and that the beloved is, thus, something that can be possessed. At some level, however, the speaker seems to feel the
inapplicability of commercial and legal concepts, and he tries to re-
solve his problem in the next stanza:

> Or if then thou gavest mee all,
> All was but All, which thou hadst then;
> But if in thy heart, since, there be or shall,
> New love created bee, by other men,
> Which have their stocks intire, and can in teares,
> In sighs, in oathes, and letters outbid mee,
> This new love may beget new feares,
> For, this love was not vowed by thee.
> And yet it was, thy gift being generall,
> The ground, thy heart is mine, what ever shall
>   Grow there, deare, I should have it all.
>   (1:17)

Troubled by his implicit knowledge that a love acquired by pur-
chase or contract cannot be securely held, the speaker here engages in
desperate intellectual strategems to coerce the beloved and to reassure

himself. The witty resolution in the last three lines of the stanza seems for a moment to be adequate, but the final stanza effects a brilliant reversal, abandoning the language of commerce and replacing it with the language of religious experience:

> Yet I would not have all yet,
> Hee that hath all can have no more,
> And since my love doth every day admit
> New growth, thou shouldst have new rewards in store;
> Thou canst not every day give me thy heart,
> If thou canst give it, then thou never gavest it:
> Loves riddles are, that though thy heart depart,
> It stayes at home, and thou with losing savest it:
> But wee will have a way more liberall,
> Than changing hearts, to joyne them, so wee shall
>   Be one, and one anothers All.
>
> (1:17–18)[7]

The great paradox central to Christianity and the other great religions—that one gains one's life by losing it—supplies the model by which the lover understands the nature of his own desire. This is not to say that the poem is a religious allegory or that it is an attempted elevation of amorous experience to the status of divine: it is rather that a part of the poem's meaning is a recognition of the basis shared by all transcendent desire (in the words of Arnold Stein, in commenting on this poem, "the love of the finite for the infinite").[8]

"Lovers Infinitenesse" dramatizes the speaker's progression to a final point of view significantly different from his initial position; and its profundity derives from the skill with which transcendent values are made to replace commercial and mundane. It is a poem rich in psychological insight. The lyric "The Anniversarie" (not to be confused with the two long poems by Donne called the "First Anniversarie" and the "Second Anniversarie") is also a brilliant display of psychological insight and subtlety, but it presents no progression of point of view:

> All Kings, and all their favorites,
>   All glory of honors, beauties, wits,
> The Sun it selfe, which makes times, as they passe,
> Is elder by a yeare, now, than it was
> When thou and I first one another saw:

All other things, to their destruction draw,
   Only our love hath no decay;
This, no to morrow hath, nor yesterday,
Running it never runs from us away,
But truly keepes his first, last, everlasting day.

   Two graves must hide thine and my coarse,
     If one might, death were no divorce.
Alas, as well as other Princes, wee,
(Who Prince enough in one another bee,)
Must leave at last in death, these eyes, and eares,
Oft fed with true oathes, and with sweet salt teares;
   But soules where nothing dwells but love
(All other thoughts being inmates) then shall prove
This, or a love increased there above,
When bodies to their graves, soules from their graves remove.

   And then wee shall be throughly blest,
     But wee no more, then all the rest;
Here upon earth, we'are Kings, and none but wee
Can be such Kings, nor of such subjects bee;
Who is so safe as wee? where none can doe
Treason to us, except one of us two.
   True and false feares let us refraine,
Let us love nobly, and live, and adde againe
Yeares and yeares unto yeares, till we attaine
To write threescore: this is the second of our raigne.

                             (1:24–25)

This appears on first reading to be another of the exalted poems in
which Donne confidently affirms the absolutely constant and transcendent nature of a true love. The obsessive imagery of the lovers as
monarchs recurs several times, and the speaker asserts not only that
the love he shares with his beloved is wholly permanent but also that
it is unique upon earth: after death, the lovers will share bliss with
the rest of the blessed in Heaven, thus losing the uniqueness that
they possess on earth. It is paradoxically implied that earth is better.
It would seem that hyperbole—and confidence—can go no further,
but, as I have argued elsewhere, a careful reading reveals that the
poem undercuts itself.[9]
    It is not only that the speaker protests too much. There are several
clues that indicate the panic, insecurity, and fear underlying his
boasts: the claim of uniqueness in stanza 1 seems rather ill-founded

in view of the recognition that *all* other things on earth "to their destruction draw"; the rhetorical question in lines 25–26—"Who is so safe as we? where none can doe / Treason to us, except one of us two"—serves rather to remind us that nothing on earth is more unsafe. In the next line the speaker lets this distressing knowledge rise almost to his consciousness: "True and false feares let us refraine"— if there *are* such things as "true feares," his confidence is unjustified, however much he may try to hide that fact.

Even the versification of the poem underlines the insecurity that is its covert subject. The last four lines of each stanza rhyme, and the lines increase progressively in length, from tetrameter to two lines of pentameter to the hyperextended final line in hexameter; the effect is one of precariousness, rather as if one were trying to pile empty beer cans one on top of the other—one would sense that sooner or later they would tumble. And, the final line of the poem reminds us, the love affair is just one year old: they have not been at it really long enough to justify the confidence protested.

Constancy/inconstancy is one of Donne's great lyric themes, whether in the ringing affirmations of constancy, the cynical praises of inconstancy, the subtle dramatization of the frightened aspiration toward constancy, or the bleakly bitter admissions that constancy cannot be found in earthly love. The last category is typified by such lyrics as "A Jeat Ring Sent" or "A Lecture upon the Shadow" with its despairing final couplet: "Love is a growing, or full constant light; / And his first minute, after noone, is night" (1:72).

Lovers' parting is another of the lyric themes to which Donne gives varied and memorable expression. One genre employed to express this theme is the *alba,* or *aubade*—the "dawn-song," introduced by the troubadours, in which the lovers must part because the approaching dawn will reveal their love to an unsympathetic or hostile world (both Shakespeare, in *Romeo and Juliet,* and Wagner, in *Tristan und Isolde,* also employed the genre to good effect). One of Donne's *aubades,* "The Sunne Rising," has already been discussed; its companion piece, "Breake of Day," is uttered through the persona of the female lover— evidence, if any more were required, of the radically dramatic and fictive nature of Donne's approach as a lyric poet.

Valedictory Poems

Walton tells us that "A Valediction: Forbidding Mourning" was composed on the occasion of one of the poet's frequent partings from

his wife in order to go on voyages required by his profession.[10] If he
is right, it is at least conceivable that all four of the "valediction"
poems of the *Songs and Sonets* have a similar occasion—and other of
the lyrics as well. "A Valediction: of My Name, in the Window" and
"A Valediction: Of the Booke" are striking combinations of extravagant and ingenious wit with turbulent passion; "A Valediction: Of
Weeping" adds to those qualities an ineffable element of tenderness.
It begins with a conceit identifying the tears of the departing lover
first with coins, bearing the reflected image of the beloved, then, by
extension, with pregnant women:

>   Let me powre forth
> My teares before thy face, whil'st I stay here,
> For thy face coines them, and thy stampe they beare,
> And by this Mintage they are something worth,
>   For thus they bee
>   Pregnant of thee;
> Fruits of much griefe they are, emblemes of more,
> When a teare falls, that thou falst which it bore,
> So thou and I are nothing then, when on a divers shore.
>
> (1:38)

The second stanza applies a new twist to Donne's familiar obsessive
image of the two lovers as constituting their own world: the tears are
like blank spheres on which a workman may paste a map of the
world:

>   On a round ball
> A workman that hath copies by, can lay
> An Europe, Afrique, and an Asia,
> And quickly make that, which was nothing, *All,*
>   So doth each teare,
>   Which thee doth weare,
> A globe, yea world by that impression grow,
> Till thy teares mixt with mine doe overflow
> This world, by waters sent from thee, my heaven dissolved so.
>
> (1:38)

And the final stanza beseeches an end to sighs and tears, urging the
old belief that each sigh shortens one's life and complicating it with
the contention that, since each lover has become the other, sighs from
one shorten the other's life:

O more then Moone,
Draw not up seas to drowne me in thy spheare,
Weepe me not dead, in thine armes, but forbeare
To teach the sea, what it may doe too soone;
    Let not the winde
    Example finde,
To doe me more harme, then it purposeth;
Since thou and I sigh one anothers breath,
Who e'r sighes most, is cruellest, and hasts the others death.
                                                        (1:39)

The imagery, theme, and tone of that last stanza are parelleled in another poem of parting, the song "Sweetest love, I do not goe," a poem which, in its regularity of meter and smoothness of diction, belies the charge that Donne is invariably irregular or even harsh in his versification:

Sweetest love, I do not goe,
    For weariness of thee,
Nor in hope the world can show
    A fitter Love for mee;
    But since that I
Must dye at last, 'tis best,
To use my selfe in jest
    Thus by fain'd deaths to dye.
                                        (1:18)

The last two stanzas recapitulate the concerns of the "Valediction: Of Weeping":

When thou sigh'st, thou sigh'st not winde,
    But sigh'st my soule away,
When thou weep'st, unkindly kinde,
    My lifes blood doth decay.
        It cannot bee
That thou lov'st mee, as thou say'st,
If in thine my life thou waste,
    That art the best of mee.

Let not thy divining heart
    Forethinke me any ill,
Destiny may take thy part,
    And may thy feares fulfill;

> But thinke that wee
> Are but turn'd aside to sleepe;
> They who one another keepe
> Alive, ne'r parted bee.
>
> (1:19)

Unusually sweet and gentle for a Donne poem, this song has nonetheless its share of complexity. In line 27, for example, the phrase "unkindly kinde" has the various meanings "unnaturally natural," "unaffectionately affectionate," "unnaturally affectionate," and "unaffectionately natural"—and it has them all at once.

The best-known of the "valediction" poems is the "Valediction: Forbidding Mourning," largely because it contains what is probably the best-known English example of the Metaphysical conceit—the one in which Donne compares the parting lovers to the two legs of a compass as it describes a circle (again, the traditional symbol of perfection). That celebrated conceit is actually introduced by another, scarcely less remarkable for its concentrated and brilliant wit:

> Our two soules therefore, which are one,
> Though I must goe, endure not yet
> A breach, but an expansion,
> Like gold to ayery thinnesse beate.
>
> (1:50)

The poets of the High Renaissance had been fond of gold as an image in the limited stock considered decorous for love poetry. In their usage the image was exploited for its yellow color (traditionally that of the beloved's hair), its brightness and shininess, and its obvious association with value and desirability. The value association is present—at least minimally—in Donne's deployment, but the principal function of the gold image in context is its chemical property of malleability. Similarly, in the great conceit of the compass (which follows immediately), the basis of comparison between tenor (the lovers) and vehicle (the legs of the compass) is nothing sensuous or physical but rather an intellectually perceptible resemblance of function:

> If they be two, they are two so
> As stiffe twin compasses are two,
> Thy soule the fixt foot, makes no show
> To move, but doth, if the'other doe.

> And though it in the center sit,
>   Yet when the other far doth rome,
> It leanes, and hearkens after it,
>   And growes erect, as that comes home.
>
> Such wilt thou be to mee, who must
>   Like th'other foot, obliquely runne;
> Thy firmnes makes my circle just,
>   And makes me end, where I begunne.
>   (1:50–51)

A special version of the poem of parting is *Elegie* XVI, one of the later elegies. In this poem the speaker, about to leave on a trip to the Continent, expostulates with his mistress, who has expressed the intention of accompanying him disguised as a page boy. The opening lines, with their reference to the "fathers wrath," suggest the possibility that the poem is addressed to Donne's wife:

> By our first strange and fatall interview,
> By all desires which thereof did ensue,
> By our long starving hopes, by that remorse
> Which my words masculine perswasive force
> Begot in thee, and by the memory
> Of hurts, which spies and rivals threatened me,
> I calmly beg: But by thy fathers wrath,
> By all paines, which want and divorcement hath,
> I conjure thee. . .
> ....
> Thou shalt not love by wayes so dangerous.
> Temper, ô faire Love, loves impetuous rage,
> Be my true Mistris still, not my faign'd Page.
>   (1:111)

With much xenophobic ingenuity, the speaker outlines the risks the beloved would run among the lustful foreigners—who would, he maintains, not be deceived by her disguise:

> All will spie in thy face
> A blushing womanly discovering grace;
> Richly cloth'd Apes, are call'd Apes, and as soone
> Ecclips'd as bright we call the Moone the Moone.
>   (1:112)

The passage includes a striking example of the typically baroque device of the diminishing metaphor, in which there is a radical discrepancy between the value implications of the tenor (in this case, the beloved) and the vehicle (the apes). As in other varieties of the metaphysical conceit, the relationship between the terms of the metaphor is one of intellectually apprehensible function rather than of physical similarity.

Elegie XVI concludes in a manner unusual for Donne—with the attribution to his mistress of a dream vision quasi-mythic in its lineaments of darkness, snow, mountains, and violent death:

> When I am gone, dreame me some happinesse,
> Nor let thy lookes our long hid love confesse,
> Nor praise, nor dispraise me, nor blesse nor curse
> Openly loves force, nor in bed fright thy Nurse
> With midnights startings, crying out, oh, oh
> Nurse, ô my love is slaine, I saw him goe
> O'r the white Alpes alone; I saw him I,
> Assail'd, fight, taken, stabb'd, bleed, fall, and die.
> Augure me better chance, except dread *Jove*
> Thinke it enough for me to'have had thy love.
>
> (1:112–13)

"A Nocturnall Upon S. *Lucies* Day"

The last of the poems of parting is concerned with the last of earthly partings, death. Its title is "A Nocturnall upon S. *Lucies* Day, Being the Shortest Day," and it is one of the most puzzling of the *Songs and Sonets*. It begins with the evocation of a grief so terrible that it has reduced its victim to a condition of total negation, virtual nonexistence; the time, appropriately, is the shortest day of the year:

> Tis the yeares midnight, and it is the dayes,
> *Lucies,* who scarce seaven houres herself unmaskes,
>   The Sunne is spent, and now his flasks
>   Send forth light squibs, no constant rayes;
>   The worlds whole sap is sunke:
> The generall balme th'hydroptique earth hath drunke,
> Whither, as to the beds-feet, life is shrunke,
> Dead and enterr'd; yet all these seeme to laugh,
> Compar'd with mee, who am their Epitaph.
>
> (1:44)

The sun is presented metaphorically as an alchemical vessel the contents of which no longer emit transformative or life-giving powers, and, presumably as a result, the vital juices of the earth itself have withdrawn into the center, like the life of a dying man ebbing toward his feet. Yet this deathly winter is downright cheerful compared to the speaker of the poem.

The second stanza elaborates the mood, develops the hyperbole, and continues the alchemical imagery:

> Study me then, you who shall lovers bee
> At the next world, that is, at the next Spring:
>   For I am every dead thing,
>   In whom love wrought new Alchimie.
>   For his art did expresse
> A quintessence even from nothingnesse,
> From dull privations, and leane emptinesse:
> He ruin'd mee, and I am re-begot
> Of absence, darknesse, death; things which are not.
>   (1:44)

According to Paracelsus the *quintessence,* or fifth element, was present in all matter. Its extraction, the goal of Paracelsian alchemy, would make possible remarkable cures as well as the transmutation of metals. Such alchemy aims at the extracting of the essence of substance; love, as alchemist, has extracted the essence of nothingness (absence, darkness, death, and similar concepts have, in scholastic philosophy, no positive existence, as they are to be conceived only as the nonpresence of their opposites—presence, light, life, etc.), and that essence is the speaker, reduced to this condition by bereavement.

> All others, from all things, draw all that's good,
> Life, soule, forme, spirit, whence they beeing have;
>   I, by loves limbecke, am the grave
>   Of all, that's nothing. Oft a flood
>   Have wee two wept, and so
> Drownd the whole world, us two; oft did we grow
> To be two Chaosses, when we did show
> Care to ought else; and often absences
> Withdrew our soules, and made us carcasses.
>   (1:44)

The speaker's condition of absolute negativity is, then, the result of a parting, and the imagery applied to that parting—familiar from the "valediction" poems, most particularly the "Valediction: Of Weeping"—suggests strongly that the absent partner is the one addressed in those poems.

The next stanza makes it clear that the parting is, this time, the permanent parting of death:

> But I am by her death, (which word wrongs her)
> Of the first nothing, the Elixer grown;
>   Were I a man, that I were one,
>   I needs must know; I should preferre,
>   If I were any beast,
> Some ends, some means; Yea plants, yea stones detest,
> And love; All, all some properties invest;
> If I an ordinary nothing were,
> As shadow, a light, and body must be here.
>   (1:45)

And the last stanza looks forward to the only reunion now to be hoped for:

> But I am None; nor will my Sunne renew.
> You lovers, for whose sake, the lesser Sunne
>   At this time to the Goat is runne
>   To fetch new lust, and give it you,
>   Enjoy your summer all;
> Since shee enjoyes her long nights festivall,
> Let mee prepare towards her, and let mee call
> This houre her Vigill, and her Eve, since this
> Both the yeares, and the dayes deep midnight is.
>   (1:45)

It seems to me virtually certain that the poem was composed as a result of the death of Donne's wife in 1617, and that it is the poet's final farewell to her. Grierson's suggestion[11] that the poem refers to Lucy, Countess of Bedford, and that the occasion is the serious illness of that noblewoman seems scarcely tenable: what the poem is talking about is not an illness, but—unmistakably—a death. And the language and imagery of the poem resemble not those of "The Funerall," "The Relique," "The Primrose," "The Undertaking," and other

poems of Platonic compliment to great ladies, but rather those of the
most passionate and intimate of Donne's love lyrics.

Other critics have assumed a relationship between Ann Donne and
the "Nocturnall," but some have assumed that the occasion was not
Ann's death in 1617 but rather a serious illness earlier in the century. [12] The assumption has, of course, to do with the earlier belief
that all Donne's amorous poetry had to have been written before
1610, at the very latest. There is no valid basis for such a belief. Even
some of those who recognize at least the possibility that the "Nocturnall" is a funerary poem for the poet's wife feel compelled to justify
such an ascription—as does, for example, Louis L. Martz, who feels
that the "Nocturnall" is essentially a religious poem. [13] It seems to me
that this work is, simultaneously, an amorous poem and a religious
poem—as is the related sonnet, the very late "Since she whom I lov'd
hath payd her last debt."

Donne's Tone

For all its difficulty, the "Nocturnall" is relatively straightforward
in its tone, as a direct expression of grief and love. Some other of the
most memorable of the *Songs and Sonets* are problematic precisely in
the matter of tone. "Loves Growth" is both passionate and tender in
tone, and it is atypical of Donne in that it utilizes nature imagery,
albeit minimally:

> I scarce beleeve my love to be so pure
>   As I had thought it was,
>   Because it doth endure
> Vicissitude, and season, as the grasse;
> Me thinkes I lyed all winter, when I swore,
> My love was infinite, if spring make'it more.
> But if this medicine, love, which cures all sorrow
> With more, not onely bee no quintessence,
> But mixt of all stuffes, paining soule, or sense,
> And of the Sunne his working vigour borrow,
> Love's not so pure, and abstract, as they use
> To say, which have no Mistresse but their Muse,
> But as all else, being elemented too,
> Love sometimes would contemplate, sometimes do.
>   (1:34)

The analysis of amorous passion via learned metaphors is familiar
from many other of Donne's lyrics, and it continues throughout the
remaining two stanzas of the poem. The concluding four lines, however, introduce an image that seems puzzlingly inappropriate in its
mundane and even cynical associations:

> If, as in water stir'd more circles bee
> Produc'd by one, love such additions take,
> Those like so many spheares, but one heaven make,
> For, they are all concentrique unto thee;
> And though each spring doe adde to love new heate,
> As princes doe in times of action get
> New taxes, and remit them not in peace,
> No winter shall abate the springs encrease.

> (1:34)

What is involved is another example of diminishing metaphor: the
comparison between love increased in springtime but remaining per-
manently at its enhanced level, and taxes increased in wartime but
remaining at their enhanced level after the coming of peace, seems so
inappropriate as to be perverse. The point, I think, is to force on the
reader an emotional response that is refracted through the intellect
rather than through the senses: the mode of operation of love and
taxes is the same, and that is all that, in context, concerns the poet.

"Aire and Angels"

Even more startling is the figure that concludes "Aire and Angels."
The entire poem follows:

> Twice or thrice had I loved thee,
> Before I knew thy face or name,
> So in a voice, so in a shapelesse flame,
> *Angells* affect us oft, and worship'd bee;
>   Still when, to where thou wert, I came,
> Some lovely glorious nothing I did see.
>   But since my soule, whose child love is,
> Takes limmes of flesh, and else could nothing doe,
>   More subtile then the parent is,
> Love must not be, but take a body too,
>   And therefore what thou wert, and who,

I bid Love aske, and now
That it assume thy body, I allow,
And fixe it selfe in thy lip, eye, and brow.

Whilst thus to ballast love, I thought,
And so more steddily to have gone,
With wares which would sinke admiration,
I saw, I had loves pinnace overfraught,
    Ev'ry thy haire for love to worke upon
Is much too much, some fitter must be sought;
    For, nor in nothing, nor in things
Extreme, and scatt'ring bright, can love inhere;
    Then as an Angell, face, and wings
Of aire, not pure as it, yet pure doth weare,
    So thy love may be my loves spheare;
        Just such disparitie
As is twixt Aire and Angells puritie,
'Twixt womens love, and mens will ever bee.
                                        (1:22)

This notoriously difficult poem may be paraphrased roughly in the following manner: The speaker has always loved his beloved, even before meeting, or even seeing, her. When he came into her presence he realized that his love—something spiritual—must assume a body, just as its parent, his own soul, was housed in its body. The soul, like any form of spirit, must have a body to become operative, and so must that spiritual thing, his love. He therefore bids his love assume, as *its* body, the body of the beloved. Thus ends the first stanza.

At the beginning of the second stanza the speaker discovers that his love is overwhelmed by the splendor of the beloved's physical beauty—as if it were a ship in danger of capsizing because of excessive ballast. A body for his love must be found elsewhere, and that satisfactory body is to be found in the beloved's love for him—a love that is very refined, very pure, but not quite spirit. His love, then, assumes her love as its body—as an angel, in order to make itself operative in the earthly sphere, assumes a body of air, the purest material substance, but not quite spirit (cf. Tasso, *Gerusalemme liberata,* 1, 13).[14]

This is all very puzzling and, to most modern readers, very obscure. But the most puzzling aspect of the conclusion is the apparent denigration of the quality and purity of the beloved's love—a beloved who has been, throughout the poem, virtually deified. It could be seen, perhaps, as one of those virtuoso twists that thwart the reader's expectation in so many of Donne's lyrics, but I can think of no other in which the wrenching of tone is quite so marked. It has been argued[15] that the lines do not actually constitute a denigration of the beloved, and, indeed, it may be that the poem suggests that, being so far above the speaker in excellence, the woman cannot feel a love quite so pure as his, which is virtually worship.

"The Extasie"

It is a part of Donne's peculiar genius that he often leaves his readers guessing. Of none of his lyrics is this more true than of "The Extasie," which has been read variously as everything from the expression of an elevated philosophy of spiritual love to a comic-dramatic representation of a skillful young seducer doing his thing in the then-fashionable mode to a harshly moralistic satire attacking the proponents of profane love.[16] It begins by setting a scene—two lovers in a landscape, holding hands and gazing into each other's eyes, in a kind of trance of love. The setting in nature is unusual for Donne, and it may be noted that the imagery smuggles in a kind of anticipation of the sexual union that has not yet taken place (e.g., "pillow on a bed," "Pregnant banke," "reclining head"):

> Where, like a pillow on a bed,
>   A Pregnant banke swel'd up, to rest
> The violets reclining head,
>   Sat we two, one anothers best.
> Our hands were firmly cimented
>   With a fast balme, which thence did spring,
> Our eye-beames twisted, and did thred
>   Our eyes, upon one double string;
> So to'entergraft our hands, as yet
>   Was all the meanes to make us one,
> And pictures in our eyes to get
>   Was all our propagation.
>
>   (1:51)

The topos of the lovers in a natural setting is familiar and traditional,[17] as is the conception of the two lovers as rivals in a conflict (cf. the "sweet enemy" oxymoron in Petrarch and his disciples)[18]:

> As 'twixt two equal Armies, Fate
>   Suspends uncertaine victorie,
> Our soules, (which to advance their state,
>   Were gone out,) hung 'twixt her, and mee.
> And whil'st our soules negotiate there,
>   Wee like sepulchral statues lay;
> All day, the same our postures were,
>   And wee said nothing, all the day.
>   (1:51–52)

The lovers are in an *ecstasy* (in Donne's time, a technical term for the condition of the soul during the mystical experience), and the governing fiction of the poem is that the souls are communicating in a soundless language to be understood only by someone completely purified by love. If such a third party were present, claims the speaker, he would hear the discourse of the lovers' souls:

> If any, so by love refin'd,
>   That he soules language understood,
> And by good love were growen all minde,
>   Within convenient distance stood,
> He (though he knew not which soule spake,
>   Because both meant, both spake the same)
> Might thence a new concoction take,
>   And part farre purer than he came.
>   (1:52)

The "dialogue of one" uttered by the two lovers makes up the rest of the poem:

> This Extasie doth unperplex
>   (We said) and tell us what we love,
> Wee see by this, it was not sexe,
>   Wee see, we saw not what did move:
> But as all severall soules containe
>   Mixture of things, they know not what,
> Love, these mixt soules doth mix againe,
>   And makes both one, each this and that.

(The *OED* cites this as the earliest recorded instance of the use of the word *sex* to refer generally to an activity rather than referring simply to "male sex" or "female sex.")[19]

> A single violet transplant,
>   The strength, the colour, and the size,
> (All which before was poore, and scant,)
>   Redoubles still, and multiplies.
>   (1:52)

It is typical of Donne to use the violet image not for its associations of color, sweet odor, hiddenness of location, or brevity of life, but rather for what the intellect may analytically observe of its behavior when transplanted.

> When love, with one another so
>   Interinanimates two soules,
> That abler soule, which thence doth flow,
>   Defects of lonelinesse controules.
> Wee then, who are this new soule, know,
>   Of what we are compos'd, and made,
> For, th'Atomies of which we grow,
>   Are soules, whom no change can invade.
>   (1:52)

The passage that follows this confident assertion of the completeness of the spiritual union has occasioned the most controversy over the proper interpretation of the poem:

> But O alas, so long, so farre
>   Our bodies why do wee forbeare?
> They'are ours, though they'are not wee, Wee are
>   The intelligences, they the spheare.
> We owe them thankes, because they thus,
>   Did us, to us, at first convey,
> Yeelded their forces, sense, to us,
>   Nor are drosse to us, but allay.

("Intelligences" in the fourth of the lines quoted above refers to the angels believed to be in charge of each of the spheres revolving about the earth.)

> On man heavens influence workes not so,
>   But that it first imprints the ayre,
> Soe soule into the soule may flow,
>   Though it to body first repaire.

> As our blood labours to beget
>   Spirits, as like soules as it can,
> Because such fingers need to knit
>   That subtile knot, which makes us man:
> So must pure lovers soules descend
>   T'affections, and to faculties,
> Which sense may reach and apprehend,
>   Else a great Prince in prison lies.
>
>   (1:53)

("Spirits" in the sixth line above has a special physiological meaning, referring to the delicate vapors believed to arise from the blood within the human body and to constitute the vital link between body and soul.)

Most commentators have read this latter part of the poem as an expression—the most complete within his entire oeuvre—of Donne's theory of love, which holds that love is an experience of the union of souls, but at the same time an experience requiring the union of bodies as the outward sign of love's completeness. Such is, it seems to me, the plain meaning of the lines—if such a delicate and subtle poem may be said to have a "plain" meaning. Some distinguished critics have, however, read it quite differently. Pierre Legouis argues the position referred to above—that the poem is a comic and dramatic enactment of a skillful and ingenious seduction. Others maintain that the lines constitute not a persuasion to physical love but simply a suggestion that the lovers return from their spiritual trance to their normal human physical condition, and some go so far as to hold that the entire poem is—as previously noted—a harshly moralistic satire.[20]

One of Donne's critics has seen the entire poem as being concerned not centrally with love at all but rather with the nature of the "subtle knot" which, joining body and soul, defines our humanity.[21] It seems to me that "The Extasie"—a seduction poem, to be sure, but one both serious and elevated—aspires to the full human condition, body united with soul, not merely in order to meditate upon it but also to do something with it. Donne writes in "Loves Growth" "Love sometimes would contemplate, sometimes do," and he says much the same thing in the concluding lines of "The Extasie":

> To'our bodies turne wee then, that so
>   Weake men on love reveal'd may looke;
> Loves mysteries in soules doe grow,

> But yet the body is his booke.
> And if some lover, such as wee,
>   Have heard this dialogue of one,
> Let him still marke us, he shall see
>   Small change, when we'are to bodies gone.
>
> (1:53)

It seems almost certain that a great many of Donne's love lyrics were written after 1600, some perhaps as late as 1617. Ben Jonson, it is true, told Drummond of Hawthornden that Donne had "written all his best pieces ere he was twenty-five years old"—which would establish 1598 as a terminal date for his lyrics—but internal evidence indicates a later date for several of the *Songs and Sonets,* and Jonson's judgment of what Donne's "best pieces" are is demonstrably different from that of posterity. [22]

During the period from 1600 to his ordination in 1615, Donne wrote in a variety of genres other than the lyric—verse letters, epithalamia, funerary poems, devotional poems, and some elegies. He also wrote several important prose works. The next chapter will consider a number of these writings.

Chapter Five
Mid-Period Poetry and Prose

The years between 1601 and 1615 were extremely difficult for John and Ann Donne. Children came one after another, there was much illness, and there was never enough money. Sir George More, recovering to some degree from his initial apoplectic reaction to his daughter's marriage, had besought the Lord Keeper to reengage his brilliant former secretary, but Sir Thomas—though with regret—declined "to discharge and re-admit servants at the request of passionate petitioners."[1] Sir George, as noted earlier, relented enough to provide his son-in-law with a modest stipend, but financial demands continued to be unceasing. Having long since spent his patrimony, Donne was forced to rely on the charity of friends and the gifts of patrons—which latter he sought assiduously with flattering verses.

After 1609 the poet's fortunes took a moderate turn for the better, friends having become more prosperous and patrons more generous. After *Pseudo-Martyr* in 1610 he enjoyed a considerable reputation as a controversialist; that work, as we have seen, attracted the favorable, though initially not very helpful, attention of King James I. It was not until his ordination in 1615 that Donne achieved financial security and the freedom to write without a thought for material gain.

For material gain is the motive inspiring the majority of the poetical works produced during this period—extravagantly complimentary verse letters addressed to great ladies and powerful noblemen, epithalamia, funerary poems of various sorts. Motive is not, however, an element germane to aesthetic worth: even the most frigid, elaborate, and, one suspects, insincere of these performances have occasional moments of sparkling brilliance, profound insight, or deeply moving eloquence. And the *Anniversaries,* built upon impossibly extravagant praise of the recently deceased daughter of one of Donne's most important patrons, constitute—whatever their motive—one of his greatest poetic achievements, a monument of English baroque poetry.

Later Elegies and Epithalamia

In addition to whatever of the *Songs and Sonets* belong to this period, five of the *Elegies* were also written after 1601. Of these, the most important are IX, XVI, (discussed in Chap. 4) and XIX. *Elegies* IX and XIX make an interesting study in contrast: IX, one of the gentlest of Donne's poems, is a tribute to friendship between a man and a woman; XIX is the most passionately physical of his erotic poems. Modern scholars accept Walton's assertion[2] that *Elegie* IX, subtitled "The Autumnall," was addressed to Lady Danvers—the former Magdalen Herbert, mother of the poet George Herbert and the poet and philosopher Edward, Lord Herbert of Cherbury, and Donne's great Platonic friend. The entire poem is dedicated to defending the proposition that love for an aging woman is more rewarding than love for a young beauty, and it is composed essentially of a series of witty and varied statements of the same apparent paradox. It begins with a memorable couplet followed by the first few of his several metaphorical illustrations:

> No *Spring,* nor *Summer* Beauty hath such grace,
>   As I have seen in one *Autumnall* face.
> Young *Beauties* force our love, and that's a *Rape,*
>   This doth but *counsaile,* yet you cannot scape.
> If t'were a *shame* to love, here t'were no *shame,*
>   *Affection* here takes *Reverences* name.
> Were her first yeares the *Golden Age;* that's true,
>   But now shee's *gold* oft tried, and ever new.
> That was her torrid and inflaming time,
>   This is her tolerable *Tropique clyme.*
>
>   (1:93)

And so on to the ineffably tender concluding lines:

> Since such loves naturall lation is, may still
>   My love descend, and journey downe the hill,
> Not panting after growing beauties, so,
>   I shall ebbe out with them, who home-ward goe.
>   (1:94)

Elegie XIX is a very different matter indeed:

> Come, madam, come, all rest my powers defie,
> Until I labour, I in labour lie.
> The foe oft-times having the foe in sight,
> Is tir'd with standing though he never fight.
>   (1:119)

The familiar oxymoron of the beloved enemy is here given a blatantly physical interpretation; the witty reference to the speaker's erection is an overt allusion to sexuality atypical of Donne, whose love poetry is, if always passionate, seldom concerned with naming externals. By the same token, the lines that follow have a descriptive vividness not often encountered in this poet's work:

> Off with that girdle, like heavens Zone glittering,
> But a far fairer world incompassing.
> Unpin that spangled breastplate which you wear,
> That th'eyes of busie fooles may be stopt there.
> Unlace your self, for that harmonious chyme [i.e., a chiming watch],
> Tells me from you, that now it is bed time.
> Off with that happy busk, which I envie,
> That still can be, and still can stand so nigh.
> Your gown going off, such beautious state reveals,
> As when from flowry meads th'hills shadow steales.
> Off with that wyerie Coronet and show
> The haiery Diademe which on you doth grow:
> Now off with those shooes, and then safely tread
> In this loves hallow'd temple, this soft bed.
>
> (1:120)

In the second verse paragraph of the elegy, vivid description modulates into a detailed sexuality that has few parallels in seventeenth-century poetry—even in the quite distinguished pornography of that age:

> Licence my roaving hands, and let them go,
> Before, behind, between, above, below.
> O my America! My new-found-land,
> My kingdome, safeliest when with one man man'd,
> My Myne of precious stones, My Emperie,
> How blest am I in this discovering thee!
> To enter in these bonds, is to be free;
> Then where my hand is set, my seal shall be.
>
> (1:120–21)

"Discovering" in line 30 is a pun, as the verb "to discover" may mean either what Columbus did to America or what one does to a person one undresses—i.e., "dis-cover." And line 32 incorporates Donne's familiar pun on "seal" as a term for the sexual organ. "Myne" is, of course, also a pun—as in "The Sunne Rising."

The third paragraph continues the praise of eroticism, effecting at
the same time a striking and altogether typical fusion of that eroticism with religious experience—more specifically, the experience of
the religious mystic, who must undergo the loss of the body in order
to be able to be vouchsafed the beatific vision, the direct beholding
of God. Here, the undressing of the mistress corresponds to the loss
of the body, while the vision of her naked body corresponds to the
vision of the Deity:

> Full nakedness! All joyes are due to thee,
> As souls unbodied, bodies uncloth'd must be,
> To taste whole joyes. Gems which you women use
> Are like Atlanta's balls, cast in mens views,
> That when a fools eye lighteth on a Gem,
> His earthly soul may covet theirs, not them.
> Like pictures, or like books gay coverings made
> For lay-men, are all women thus array'd;
> Themselves are mystick books, which only wee
> (Whom their imputed grace will dignifie)
> Must see reveal'd. Then since that I may know;
> As liberally, as to a Midwife, shew
> Thy self: cast all, yea, this white lynnen hence,
> There is no pennance due to innocence.
> To teach thee, I am naked first; why than
> What needst thou have more covering then a man.
>
> (1:121)

A notable feature of the poem is its strongly genital orientation. In
more traditional love poetry—such as most of that of the Renaissance—it is the lady's secondary sexual characteristics that get the
most attention, and the most loving attention—breasts, neck, eyes,
hair, etc. For Donne, as the reference to the midwife suggests, it is
the genitalia that are of paramount, almost exclusive importance. He
makes this point overtly in the closing lines of *Elegie* XVIII:

> Rich Nature hath in women wisely made
> Two purses, and their mouths aversely laid:
> They then, which to the lower tribute owe,
> That way which that Exchequer looks, must go:
> He which doth not, his error is as great,
> As who by Clyster gave the Stomack meat.
>
> (1:119)

The three epithalamia of Donne's middle period are neither so explicit nor so bawdy. The first of these wedding poems, composed during Donne's years as a law student at Lincoln's Inn, has already been cited. The second was written on the occasion of the marriage of King James's daughter, the princess Elizabeth, to the count Palatine on Valentine's Day, 1613. (The ill-fated pair were destined to become king and queen of Bohemia for one brief winter, after which they were driven into exile during the fury of the Thirty Years' War.) The remaining epithalamium, in the form of an eclogue followed by the hymn proper, had a rather scandalous occasion—the marriage of James's favorite, the earl of Somerset, to the former countess of Essex, who had, in furtherance of her adulterous affair with Somerset, managed to achieve an annulment of her marriage. The marriage to Somerset took place in 1613. The circumstances of this intrigue in no sense discouraged Donne from writing a richly harmonious and curiously innocent celebration. But, then, as Donne remarked in a letter, he "always did best when [he] had least truth for [his] subject."

Epistles

Neither the verse letters of this period nor the funerary poems are very deeply rooted in truth, a fact that does not diminish their artistic worth, given the aesthetic assumptions of the age. One of the many epistles to Lucy, countess of Bedford, may serve to exemplify certain of the qualities of these poems. It is the poem beginning "Honour is so sublime perfection," and it was probably written in around 1612. It opens with a disquisition on the nature of honor, demonstrating that honor is bestowed by the inferior on the superior and thereby justifying his intended praise of the countess:

> Honour is so sublime perfection,
> And so refinde; that when God was alone
> And creaturelesse at first, himselfe had none;
>
> But as of the elements, those which wee tread,
> Produce all things with which wee'are joy'd or fed,
> And, those are barren both above our head:
>
> So from low persons doth all honour flow;
> Kings, whom they would have honoured, to us show,
> And but *direct* our honour, not *bestow*.

> For when from herbs the pure part must be wonne
> From grosse, by Stilling [i.e., distilling] this is better done
> By despis'd dung, then by the fire or Sunne.
>
> Care not then, Madame, 'how low your praysers lye;
> In labourers balads oft more piety
> God findes, then in *Te Deums* melodie.
>
> And, ordinance rais'd on Towers, so many mile
> Send not their voice, nor last so long a while
> As fires from th'earths low vaults in *Sicil* Isle.
>
> (1:218)

In its ingenuity, its paradoxical argument, and its illustration of that argument by images drawn from obscure areas of knowledge (processes of distillation, for example, and Sicilian volcanoes), the passage is typical of Donne's practice in this kind of verse letter. One element in the genre is, of course, implicit flattery of the lady by making evident an assumption that she both follows the tortuous argument and catches the obscure allusions.

The rest of the poem is devoted to outrageous praise of the countess:

> Should I say I liv'd darker then were true,
> Your radiation can all clouds subdue;
> But one, 'tis best light to contemplate you.

(the "one" whose light exceeds Lucy's is, of course, God.)

> You, for whose body God made better clay,
> Or tooke Soules stuffe such as shall late decay,
> Or such as needs small change at the last day.
>
> This, as an Amber drop enwraps a Bee,
> Covering discovers your quicke Soule; that we
> May in your through-shine [i.e., transparent] front your hearts
>   thoughts see.
>
> You teach (though wee learne not) a thing unknowne
> To our late times, the use of specular stone,
> Through which all things within without were shown.
>
> (1:218–19)

"Specular stone" is referred to also in Donne's lyric "The Undertaking." By it is probably meant old selenite, a mineral that reputedly could be cut into transparent segments by a skill lost after ancient times.[3]

> Of such were Temples; so and of such you are;
> *Beeing* and *seeming* is your equal care,
> And *vertues* whole *summe* is but *know* and *dare.*
>
> But as our Soules of growth and Soules of sense
> Have birthright of our reasons Soule, yet hence
> They fly not from that, nor seeke presidence:
>
> Natures first lesson, so, discretion,
> Must not grudge zeale a place, nor yet keepe none,
> Not banish it selfe, nor religion.
>
> Discretion is a wisemans Soule, and so
> Religion is a Christians, and you know
> How these are one; her *yea* is not her *no.*
>
> Nor may we hope to sodder still and knit
> These two, and dare to breake them; nor must wit
> Be colleague to religion, but be it.
>
> In those poor types of God (round circles) so
> Religions tipes, the peecelesse centers flow,
> And are in all the lines which all wayes goe.
>
> If either ever wrought in you alone
> Or principally, then religion
> Wrought your ends, and your wayes discretion.
>
> Goe thither still, goe the same way you went,
> Who so would change, do covet or repent;
> Neither can reach you, great and innocent.
>   (1:219–20)

Some of the verse letters addressed to others are significantly different in tone. The one addressed to Magdalen Herbert—the lines beginning "Mad paper stay"—is considerably more intimate, with a combination of gaiety, affection, and innocent flirtatiousness that

keeps fresh after almost four centuries. The epistle "To Sir Edward
Herbert. At Julyers" is an amusing example of Donne's subtle humor. Sir Edward—later to become Lord Herbert of Cherbury—was
Magdalen Herbert's eldest son, and a man destined to achieve recognition as an ambassador, an autobiographer, a philosopher of some
originality, and a poet of real, if modest, talent. He was also egotisti-
cal, addicted to unacknowledged literary borrowing, fond of deliberate obscurity in poetic expression, and almost terminally frigid in his
poetic diction. The epistle is, I believe, an answer to Herbert's satire
"The State Progresse of Ill,"[4] a poem that seeks obscurity almost as
much as it courts a pose of intellectual sophistication. Herbert almost
certainly sent it to Donne in 1608 or thereabouts.[5] Donne's poem,
polite and suave, concludes with the following lines:

> All that is fill'd, and all that which doth fill,
>   All the round world, to man is but a pill,
> In all it workes not, but it is in all
>   Poysonous, or purgative, or cordiall,
> For, knowledge kindles Calentures [i.e., fevers] in some,
>   And is to others icy *Opium.*
> As brave as true, is that profession than
>   Which you do use to make; that you know man.
> This makes it credible; you have dwelt upon
>   All worthy bookes, and now are such an one.
> Actions are authors, and of those in you
>   Your friends finde everyday a mart of new.
>
>   (1:195)

The poem ends as it began, in compliment, but it is a rather
mixed compliment, suggesting as it does that knowledge, which in-
spires some people with fervent passion, makes Herbert cold, and
concluding with the amused hint that Herbert's friends find his conversation stuffed with his borrowings from authors he has read.

Funerary Poems

Ben Jonson stated that Donne had told him that he had written
his "Elegie upon the Untimely Death of the Incomparable Prince
Henry" in such a way as "to match Sir Edward Herbert in obscure-
nesse."[6] This he surely succeeded in accomplishing, in a bloated funerary poem of some ninety-eight lines. The beginning is typical of
the entire performance:

> Looke to mee faith, and looke to my faith, God;
> For both my centers feele this period.
> Of waight one center, one of greatnesse is;
> And Reason is that center, Faith is this.
>
> (1:267)

The prince whose demise is thus lamented was the eldest son of James I and his queen, Anne of Denmark, and he was thus the heir apparent to the British throne. Given not only the literary conventions of Donne's age but also its general weltanschauung, extravagant praise of such a figure is altogether in order: the virtuous prince, it may be assumed, would have brought happiness, peace, and prosperity to his people if he had lived, and lamentation for him may be altogether valid even if impersonal. But the triviality of Donne's lament is underscored by the fact that it concludes with an apostrophe to the prince's unknown and purely hypothetical beloved. This elegy offers no competition, shall we say, to Milton's "Lycidas"—a poem that makes of a lament for a dead young man only slightly known to the poet an imperishable threnody on the fact of mortality itself.

To some extent all seven of the poems grouped together in the Grierson edition as *Epicedes and Obsequies* share in the frigidity, aridity, and pointless complication of the "Elegy on Prince Henry." They are, like the *Verse Letters,* among the least frequently read of Donne's poetical works. Nevertheless, even in these poems one encounters passages that are vintage Donne in their dense concentration, their distilled grandeur—the following lines, for example, that begin the "Obsequies to the Lord Harrington, Brother to the Lady Lucy, Countesse of Bedford":

> Faire soule, which wast, not onely, as all soules bee,
> Then when thou wast infused, harmony,
> But did'st continue so; and now dost beare
> A part in Gods great organ, this whole Spheare:
> If looking up to God; or downe to us,
> Thou finde that any way is pervious,
> Twixt heav'n and earth, and that mans actions doe
> Come to your knowledge, and affections too,
> See, and with joy, mee to that good degree
> Of goodnesse growne, that I can studie thee,
> And, by these meditations refin'd,
> Can unapparell and enlarge my minde,

And so can make by this soft extasie,
This place a map of heav'n, my selfe of thee.

(1:271)

Even the "Elegy on Prince Henry" has a couple of lines that, once encountered, remain in the mind—a parenthetical description of the dead prince as "Our Soules best baiting, and midd-period, / In her long journey, of considering God" (1:270).

The "First Anniversary"

The romantic and postromantic assumption that sincerity and personal involvement are necessary preconditions for achieving greatness in poetry would seem to receive support from the relative weakness of Donne's work in the funerary and epistolary genres. Such an assumption is, however, invalidated by a consideration of the "Funerall Elegie" and the two *Anniversaries* written to lament the death of Elizabeth Drury, the fourteen-year-old daughter of Sir Robert Drury, one of Donne's principal patrons. Taken together they constitute the poet's most sustained achievement in the longer genres, his most intellectually profound poetic utterance, and one of the greatest English poems of the seventeenth century—although, by Donne's own testimony, he had never seen the girl.[7]

The "First Anniversary" was published in 1611 together with the "Funerall Elegie"; the "Second Anniversary" was published in 1612. They were the first of Donne's poems to appear in print during his lifetime.

The "First Anniversary" is subtitled "An Anatomie of the World. *Wherein,* By occasion of the untimely death of Mistris Elizabeth Drury, the frailty and the decay of this whole World is represented." This poem of 474 lines is followed in most editions by the much shorter "Funerall Elegie," and then by the "Second Anniversary," a poem of 528 lines subtitled "Of the Progresse of the Soule. *Wherein,* By occasion of the Religious death of Mistris Elizabeth Drury, the incommoditites of the Soule in this life, and her exaltation in the next, are contemplated." Earlier scholars believed that the "Funerall Elegie" was written first, followed at one-year intervals by the *Anniversaries,*[8] but there is no clear evidence for the assumption; it is equally possible that the "Funerall Elegie" and the "First Anniversarie" were composed during the same period, followed a year later by the "Second Anniversary." Like Milton's "L'Allegro" and "Il Penseroso," the *Anniversaries* are companion pieces, meant to be read as illuminating one another.

Several words appearing in Donne's long subtitles deserve attention. *Anatomie* is a technical term, with approximately the meaning of the modern term *dissection*. (It is in many ways a key term for an understanding of the preoccupations of later Renaissance and early baroque writers, as such titles as *The Anatomie of Wit* and *The Anatomie of Melancholy* suggest: it is a vital metaphor in an age preoccupied with analysis.) *Progresse* is also a kind of technical term, designating (as in the title of Lord Herbert's "Of the State Progress of Ill") an official journey undertaken by a reigning monarch, with all the ceremonial appropriate to such an occasion. Another important word, occurring in both subtitles is *occasion,* a term that implies—as several passages in the poems also suggest—that we are not to conceive of the subject of the poems in any simple or limited way, that the dead Elizabeth praised in the poems subsumes in herself many other identities. Thus, in the "First Anniversary":

Her name defin'd thee [i.e., the world, here addressed by the poem],
    gave thee forme, and frame,
And thou forgett'st to celebrate thy name
Some moneths she hath beene dead (but being dead,
Measures of times are all determined)
But long she'ath beene away, long, long, yet none
Offers to tell us who it is that's gone.

                                                    (1:232)

The reader needs all the help he or she can get. For, since their first appearance, the *Anniversaries* have been a source of perplexity, confusion, and even rage to critics. Ben Jonson maintained that "Donnes *Anniversary* was profane and full of blasphemies; that he told Mr. Done, if it had been written of the Virgin Mary, it had been something; to which he answered that he described the Idea of a Woman, and not as she was."[9] And Grierson, most sympathetic of critics, finds in the poems a "combination of what is execrable with what is magnificent, of the ingenuities of a too subtle and erudite wit irradiated by a passionate imaginative apprehension of the spiritual and transcendent, of frigidities and harshness of imagery and phrasing with felicitous and incandescent phrases and varied harmonies."[10]

What troubles Jonson, Grierson, and so many others is the apparent gross discrepancy between the dead little girl (or any conceivable mortal subject) and the fulsome praise that is lavished on her. As William Empson has remarked, "the poems make sense only if Elizabeth Drury is identified with the logos."[11] One of the triumphs of modern scholarship in English studies has been to make these difficult poems accessible to the modern reader. Before noting in detail the findings of the scholars responsible for that work, it will be necessary to rehearse the action of the poems.

The "First Anniversary" is based on the assertion that, with the death of the young girl, the world itself has died and is, in fact, in a state of decay:

> But though it be too late to succour thee,
> Sicke World, yea, dead, yea putrefied, since shee
> Thy'intrinseque balme, and thy preservative,
> Can never be renew'd, thou never live,
> I (since no man can make thee live) will try,
> What wee may gaine by thy Anatomy.
>
> (1:233)

The dissection proceeds rigorously, examining sequentially the following phenomena: (1) the impossibility of health, (2) the shortness of human life, as compared with life in patriarchal times, (3) the smallness of human stature, as compared with those times, (4) the correspondent decay of the natural environment in which humans live, as evidenced by (5) the breakdown of order and proportion in the natural world, (6) the breakdown of the moral order, and (7) the loss of color in the world, and, finally (8) the breakdown of the correspondences once believed to obtain in the cosmos—between heaven and earth, as between humanity and nature.

The ideas on which the anatomy is based are two: the myth of progressive degeneration (almost as generally received during the baroque age as the equally improbable myth of progress was during the nineteenth century), and the assumption of an initial symbolic and hierarchical order in the universe, according to which heavenly aspects correspond to those on earth, as the human body (and mind) correspond to external nature. The ideas imply each other: degeneration is demonstrated by the obvious breakdown in universal correspondence (similar ideas dominate the *Hydriotaphia, or Urn-Buriall* of Donne's somewhat younger contemporary Sir Thomas Browne). Scholarship has traced the roots of these preoccupations in many baroque authors to the disturbing implications of what was then the "new science," especially that of astronomy, and the following lines from the "First Anniversary" are often quoted as if they summarized the actual argument of the poem:

> So did the world from the first houre decay,
> That evening was beginning of the day,
> And now the Springs and Sommers which we see,
> Like sonnes of women after fiftie bee.
> And new Philosophy calls all in doubt,
> The Element of fire is quite put out;
> The Sun is lost, and th'earth, and no mans wit
> Can well direct him where to looke for it.
> And freely men confesse that this world's spent,
> When in the Planets, and the Firmament
> They seeke so many new; they see that this
> Is crumbled out againe to his Atomies.
> 'Tis all in peeces, all cohaerence gone;
> All just supply, and all Relation:
> Prince, Subject, Father, Sonne, are things forgot,
> For every man alone thinkes he hath got
> To be a Phoenix, and that then can bee
> None of that kinde, of which he is, but hee.
>   (1:237–38)

In context it is clear that the "new Philosophy" in itself has not *caused* the disintegration of the world; it has rather simply made evident the decay that was implicit from the time of the Fall in Eden onward. The poem is not about the new philosophy; it is about the death of some vital principle that had previously kept that implicit decay from establishing its dominion.

In any interpretation of the poem the reader is left with the crucial question: who is "she"? "She" is eulogized five times in the "First Anniversary," each time at the end of a stage of the dissection. The eight sections listed above may alternatively be seen as constituting five structural units: (1) the degeneration of humanity, (2) the decay of nature, (3) the loss of proportion in the world, (4) the loss of color, (5) the breakdown of universal correspondences. The eulogy following the first unit goes as follows:

She, of whom th'Ancients seem'd to prophesie,
When they call'd vertues by the name of *shee;*
Shee in whom vertue was so much refin'd,
That for Allay unto so pure a minde
Shee tooke the weaker Sex; shee that could drive
The poysonous tincture, and the staine of *Eve,*
Out of her thoughts, and deeds; and purifie
All, by a true religious Alchymie;
Shee, shee is dead; shee's dead: when thou knowest this,
Thou knowest how poore a trifling thing man is.
And learn'st thus much by our Anatomie,
The heart being perish'd, no part can be free.
And that except thou feed (not banquet [i.e., snack]) on
The supernatural food, Religion,
Thy better Growth growes withered, and scant;
Be more then man, or thou'rt lesse then an Ant.
                                                    (1:236–37)

It is thus affirmed that the dead girl was the soul of the human race,
its better part; the second eulogy (immediately following the "new
philosophy" passage) makes of her the soul of the world itself:

This is the worlds condition now, and now
She that should all parts to reunion bow,
She that had all Magnetique force alone,
To draw, and fasten sundred parts in one;
She whom wise nature had invented then
When she observ'd that every sort of men
Did in their voyage in the worlds Sea stray,
And needed a new compasse for their way;
She that was best, and first originall
Of all faire copies, and the generall
Steward to Fate; she whose rich eyes, and brest
Guilt the West Indies, and perfum'd the East;
Whose having breath'd in this world, did bestow
Spice on those Iles, and bad them still smell so,
And that rich Indie which doth gold interre,
Is but as single money, coyn'd from her:
She to whom this world must it selfe refer,
As Suburbs, or the microcosme of her,
Shee, shee is dead; shee's dead: when thou knowest this,
Thou knowst how lame a cripple this world is.
And learn'st thus much by our Anatomy,

> That this worlds generall sickenesse doth not lie
> In any humour, or one certaine part;
> But as thou sawest it rotten at the heart,
> Thou seest a Hectique feaver hath got hold
> Of the whole substance, not to be contrould,
> And that thou hast but one way, not t'admit
> The worlds infection, to be none of it.
>
> (1:238)

The concluding lines of the passage enunciate the theme *de contemptu mundi* that will become increasingly stronger and more overt in the remaining eulogies and will become the obsessive subject of the "Second Anniversary." Beauty of physical form and, next, the vivid beauty of the physical world are presented as a destroyed illusion now that the soul of that world has departed:

> Shee, after whom, what forme so'er we see,
> Is discord, and rude incongruitie;
> Shee, shee is dead, shee's dead; when thou knowest this
> Thou knowest how ugly a monster this world is:
> And learn'st thus much by our Anatomie,
> That here is nothing to enamour thee. . .
> But shee, in whom all white, and red, and blew
> (Beauties ingredients) voluntary grew,
> As in an unvext Paradise; from whom
> Did all things verdure, and their lustre come,
> Whose composition was miraculous,
> Being all colour, all Diaphanous,
> (For Ayre, and Fire but thick grosse bodies were,
> And liveliest stones but drowsie, and pale to her,)
> Shee, shee, is dead: shee's dead: when thou know'st this,
> Thou knowst how wan a Ghost this our world is:
> And learn'st thus much by our Anatomie,
> That it should more affright, then pleasure thee.
>
> (1:241–42)

A mighty effort of imagination and will is at work attempting to transform love for earthly things into love for heavenly. The effort continues even more strenuously in the "Second Anniversary," one reason that poem seems such a definitive expression of the baroque sensibility.

The last of the formal eulogies in the "First Anniversary" begins with what is perhaps the most extravagant of Donne's diminishing metaphors:

> But as some Serpents poyson hurteth not,
> Except it be from the live Serpent shot,
> So doth her vertue need her here, to fit
> That unto us; shee working more then it.

The radical discrepancy between the value implications of the tenor and those of the vehicle is singularly appropriate in the context of a work in which the validity of everything earthly is strongly rejected.

> But shee, in whom to such maturity
> Vertue was growne, past growth, that it must die;
> She, from whose influence all Impressions came,
> But, by Receivers impotencies, lame,
> Who, though she could not transubstantiate
> All states to gold, yet guilded every state,
> So that some Princes have some temperance;
> Some Counsellers some purpose to advance
> The common profit; and some people have
> Some stay, no more than Kings should give, to crave;
> Some women have some taciturnity,
> Some nunneries some graines of chastitie.
> She that did thus much, and much more could doe,
> But that our age was Iron, and rustie too,
> Shee, shee is dead; shee's dead; when thou knowst this,
> Thou knowst how drie a Cinder this world is.
> And learn'st thus much by our Anatomy,
> That 'tis in vaine to dew, or mollifie
> It with thy teares, or sweat, or blood: nothing
> Is worth our travaile, griefe, or perishing,
> But those rich joyes, which did possesse her heart,
> Of which she's now partaker, and a part.
>
> (1:243–44)

Martz has most convincingly demonstrated that the structure of the *Anniversaries* is not so much elegiac—in the manner of "Lycidas" or "Adonais"—as it is meditative, following the pattern of spiritual discipline embodied in the devotional exercises devised by Ignatius of Loyola in the middle of the sixteenth century. Ignatian meditation was of extraordinary importance for the religious writings of the seventeenth century, Protestant as well as Catholic. It was particularly important for Donne's devotional poetry, and will be discussed in more detail in the context of that work. For the present it may suffice to note that formal meditation was an intellectual discipline that enabled the meditator, bringing into play the mental faculties of memory, understanding, and will, to effect within his imagination a complete fusion of concrete image with abstract meaning and intellectual understanding with emotional involvement. Using such intellectual instruments, Donne makes his lament for the death of a little girl coextensive with a vision of the life and death of the cosmos and the soul's liberation from the body.

Martz sees the two *Anniversaries* as being of unequal aesthetic value, the first a more or less magnificent failure, the second "one of the great religious poems of the seventeenth century."[12] It would be more accurate to regard the "First Anniversary" as incomplete without the "Second," recognizing, with Marjorie Nicolson, that they constitute not two discrete poetic utterances but one—the first analyzing the death of the body, the second celebrating the liberation and glorification of the soul.[13]

"The Idea of a Woman, and not as she was," Donne's answer to Jonson's criticism of the poem, remains puzzling to scholars. In rehabilitating the *Anniversaries,* twentieth-century scholarship has been inventive and tireless in finding an identity for Donne's subject. For Nicolson, the identity of "she" is multiple, sometimes to be visualized as the Virgin Mary (the identification might have mollified Jonson), sometimes as the goddess Astraea (pagan goddess of justice, whose progressive removal from the world caused the age of gold to yield first to the age of silver and finally to the age of iron), sometimes as the recently deceased Elizabeth I (whom Donne had covertly attacked a few years before in his "Metempsychosis: The Progresse of the Soule"—the title virtually identical with the subtitle of the "Second Anniversary").[14]

Nicolson's suggestion that Elizabeth I is somehow involved in the poems has not met with much critical agreement, nor has her ingenious suggestion that the variation of spelling ("she" versus "shee") in the poems is meant to signal a shifting between Elizabeth Drury and others as subjects. Astraea and the Blessed Virgin have been viewed by other critics, however, as valid symbolic extensions of the subject matter, and to these Frank Manley, in his detailed and excel-

lent introduction to his critical edition of the poems,[15] has added a
whole dramatis personae of other identities: Aphrodite Urania, the
Angelic Mind of the Neoplatonists, Sophia or Divine Wisdom, the
Shekinah of Hebrew tradition, and, finally, the anima of Jungian
thought.

The "Second Anniversary"

The anima perhaps sums up all the identities—the idea that within
the self there is another, more central self—one that is, regardless of
one's gender, female. Its existence is suggested by the fact that the
human mind conceives of the soul as "she." The "Second Anniversary" gives expression—in numerous passages of unforgettable
beauty—to this universal human awareness. A particularly brilliant,
though unobtrusive aspect of the work is the gradual, even stealthy,
transition from the antecedent of "she" as "Elizabeth Drury," or who-
ever else, to "she" as the human soul. Relevant here is the entire tradition of *dolce stil nuovo* poetry, and its definitive renditions: Dante's
Beatrice and Petrarch's Laura as spiritual guides, leading the poets to
Paradise:

> Thirst for that time, o my insatiate soule,
> And serve thy thirst, with Gods safe-sealing Bowle.
> Be thirstie still, and drinke still till thou goe
> To th'only Health, to be Hydroptique so.
> Forget this rotten world; and unto thee
> Let thine owne times as an old storie bee.
> Be not concern'd: study not why, nor when;
> Doe not so much as not beleeve a man.
> For though to erre, be worst, to try truths forth,
> Is far more businesse, then this world is worth.
> The world is but a carkasse; thou art fed
> By it, but as a worme, that carkasse bred;
> And why should'st thou, poore worme, consider more,
> When this world will grow better then before,
> Then those thy fellow wormes doe thinke upon
> That carkasses last resurrection.
> Forget this world, and scarce thinke of it so,
> As of old clothes, cast off a yeare agoe.
> To be thus stupid is Alacritie;
> Men thus Lethargique have best Memory.
>   (1:252–53)

The structure of the "Second Anniversary" strictly parallels that of the "First Anniversary," but whereas the meditations of the first poem demonstrate, with much learning and thoroughness, the destruction of the world and lead to a recurrent refrain of lamentation for the death of its soul, the second poem meditates on the total vanity of all worldly learning, and its meditations lead to a recurrent refrain of celebration for the liberation of the soul. The refrain closely resembles that of the "First Anniversary," but with the significant substitution of the word *gone* for the word *dead:*

> Look upward; that's towards her, whose happy state
> We now lament not, but congratulate.
> Shee, to whom all this world was but a stage,
> Where all sat harkning how her youthfull age
> Should be emploi'd, because in all shee did,
> Some Figure of the Golden times was hid.
> Who could not lacke, what e'r this world could give,
> Because shee was the forme, that made it live;
> Nor could complaine, that this world was unfit
> To be staid in, then when shee was in it;
> Shee that first tried indifferent desires
> By vertue, and vertue by religious fires,
> Shee to whose person Paradise adher'd,
> As Courts to Princes, shee whose eyes ensphear'd
> Star-light enough, t'have made the South controule,
> (Had shee been there) the Star-full Northerne Pole,
> Shee, shee is gone; she is gone; when thou knowest this,
> What fragmentary rubbidge this world is
> Thou knowest, and that it is not worth a thought;
> He honors it too much that thinkes it nought.
>
> (1:253)

In this initial eulogy the subject clearly includes Elizabeth Drury, despite Nicolson's argument about the spelling of *shee,* but the identity becomes more suspect in the meditation that immediately ensues. It is a meditation on the speaker's own deathbed—a favorite subject for formal meditation—and in its course *soul* refers pretty clearly not to Elizabeth as soul of the world but to the speaker's soul—and, by extension, to anyone's soul:

> Thinke then, my soule, that death is but a Groome,
> Which brings a Taper to the outward roome,

Whence thou spiest first a little glimmering light,
And after brings it nearer to thy sight:
For such approaches doth heaven make in death.
Thinke thy selfe labouring now with broken breath,
And thinke those broken and soft Notes to bee
Division, and thy happyest Harmonie,
Thinke thee laid on thy death-bed, loose and slacke;
And thinke that, but unbinding of a packe,
To take one precious thing, thy soule from thence.
Thinke thy selfe parch'd with fevers violence,
Anger thine ague more, by calling it
Thy Physicke; chide the slacknesse of the fit.
Thinke that thou hear'st thy knell, and think no more,
But that, as Bels cal'd thee to Church before,
So this, to the Triumphant Church, calls thee.
Thinke Satans Sergeants round about thee bee,
And thinke that but for Legacies they thrust;
Give one thy Pride, to'another give thy Lust:
Give them those sinnes which they gave thee before,
And trust th'immaculate blood to wash thy score.
Thinke thy friends weeping round, and thinke that they
Weepe but because they goe not yet thy way.
Thinke that they close thine eyes, and thinke in this,
That they confesse much in the world, amisse,
Who dare not trust a dead mans eye with that,
Which they from God, and Angels cover not.
Thinke that they shroud thee up, and think from thence
They reinvest thee in white innocence.
Thinke that thy body rots, and (if so low,
Thy soule exalted so, thy thoughts can goe,)
Think thee a Prince, who of themselves create
Wormes which insensibly devoure their State.
Thinke that they bury thee, and thinke that rite
Laies thee to sleepe but a Saint Lucies night.

                                                                    (1:253–54)

   The formal meditation, as outlined by Ignatius of Loyola, consists
of three parts—the composition of place, the analysis, and the colloquy—each corresponding to one of the three powers of the soul. In
the composition of place the meditator imagines, as concretely and
circumstantially as possible, some scene—the passion of Christ perhaps, or the meditator's own deathbed. In the analysis he or she applies the intellect to the consideration of each detail, worrying it for

its symbolic significance, and usually employing extravagant metaphors in order to do so as effectively as possible. The experience of
the first two phases of the meditation leads to the final phase, the
colloquy, in which the emotions are ignited with fervor and the meditator is capable of passionate address to God, to the soul, or to some
other entity.[16]

The devotional poetry deriving from formal meditation does not
invariably recapitulate all three phases. Many of Donne's *Holy Sonnets*
are composed of the colloquy alone, the fruit of a silent meditation,
and the long passage just quoted exhibits a composition of place turning into an analysis.

The "Second Anniversary" has been much discussed as a work in
the *de contemptu mundi* tradition.[17] Operating within this tradition, the
poet heaps opprobrium on the body in a manner reminiscent of some
of the early Fathers of the Church:

> Thinke that no stubborne sullen Anchorit,
> Which fixt to a pillar, or a grave, doth sit
> Bedded, and bath'd in all his ordures, dwels
> So fowly as our Soules in their first-built Cels.
> Thinke in how poore a prison thou didst lie
> After, enabled but to suck, and crie.
> Thinke, when 'twas growne to most, 'twas a poore Inne,
> A Province pack'd up in two yards of skinne,
> And that usurp'd or threatned with the rage
> Of sicknesses, or their true mother, Age.
>
> (1:256)

There ensues immediately a brilliant description of the liberated
soul's ascent to Heaven—and, at this point, "shee" is no longer Elizabeth Drury or any other defined identity but has become rather the
soul in general:

> But thinke that Death hath now enfranchis'd thee,
> Thou hast thy'expansion now, and libertie;
> Thinke that a rustie Peece, discharg'd, is flowne
> In peeces, and the bullet is his owne,
> And freely flies: This to thy Soule allow,
> Thinke thy shell broke, thinke thy Soule hatch'd but now.
> And think this slow-pac'd soule, which late did cleave
> To'a body, and went but by the bodies leave,

Twenty, perchance, or thirty mile a day,
Dispatches in a minute all the way
'Twixt heaven, and earth; she stayes not in the ayre,
To looke what Meteors there themselves prepare;
She carries no desire to know, nor sense,
Whether th'ayres middle region be intense;
For th'Element of fire, she doth not know,
Whether she past by such a place or no;
She baits not at the Moone, nor cares to trie
Whether in that new world, men live, and die.
Venus retards her not, to'enquire, how shee
Can, (being one starre) *Hesper* and *Vesper* bee;
Hee that charm'd *Argus* eyes, sweet *Mercury,*
Workes not on her, who now is growne all eye;
Who, if she meet the body of the Sunne,
Goes through, not staying till his course be runne;
Who findes in *Mars* his Campe no corps of Guard;
Nor is by *Jove,* nor by his father barr'd;
But ere she can consider how she went,
At once is at, and through the Firmament.
And as these starres were but so many beads
Strung on one string, speed undistinguish'd leads
Her through those Spheares, as through the beads, a string,
Whose quick succession makes it still one thing:
As doth the pith, which, lest our bodies slacke,
Strings fast the little bones of necke, and backe.

                                                    (1:256–57)

In the "First Anniversary" Donne had tormented himself with his observations of the ways in which modern science had destroyed—or,
rather, revealed a self-destruction always inherent in—the order and
beauty of the world. In this passage, he remarks that it is all irrelevant. The next marginal gloss in the poem notes "Her [the soul's]
ignorance in this life and knowledge in the next," and the poem elaborates upon the remark:

        Poore soule, in this thy flesh what does thou know?
        Thou know'st thy selfe so little, as thou know'st not,
        How thou didst die, nor how thou wast begot.
        Thou neither know'st, how thou at first cam'st in,
        Nor how thou took'st the poyson of mans sinne.
        Nor dost thou, (though thou know'st, that thou art so)
        By what way thou art made immortall, know.

.   .   .   Have not all soules thought
For many ages, that our body's wrought
Of Ayre, and Fire, and other Elements?
And now they thinke of new ingredients,
And one Soule thinkes one, and another way
Another thinkes, and 'tis an even lay. . .
Wee see in Authors, too stiffe to recant,
A hundred controversies of an Ant;
And yet one watches, starves, freeses, and sweats,
To know but Catechismes and Alphabets
Of unconcerning things, matters of fact;
How others on our stage their parts did Act;
What *Caesar* did, yea, and what *Cicero* said.
Why grasse is greene, or why our blood is red,
Are mysteries which none have reach'd unto.
In this low forme, poore soule, what wilt thou doe?
When wilt thou shake off this Pedantery,
Of being taught by sense, and Fantasie?
Thou look'st through spectacles; small things seeme great
Below; but up unto the watch-towre get,
And see all things despoyl'd of fallacies:
Thou shalt not peepe through lattices of eyes,
Nor heare through Labyrinths of eares, nor learne
By circuit, or collections to discerne.
In heaven thou straight know'st all, concerning it,
And what concernes it not, shalt straight forget.

                                        (1:258–59)

One of the defining features of the baroque age is the intense preoc-cupation of its intellectuals with the investigation of the material world, an expansion of the Renaissance spirit from the realm of art to the realm of thought: the seventeenth century, after all, laid the foundations of what we know as science. For some baroque thinkers and writers the preoccupation was not psychologically problematic (even if some, like Giordano Bruno, had to pay for it with their lives): Bacon, Gilbert, Kepler, Galileo, and others found no conflict between religious faith and the scientific enterprise. Others, like Sir Thomas Browne, seem curiously split, peering, Janus-like, toward the future and toward the medieval past. Still others cannot resist the appeal of novel scientific speculation and experimentation but have a queasy conscience about it, convinced that only the invisible, the

spiritual, can have reality or value. John Donne is one of the last
group, and the *Anniversaries* constitute the major documentation of
the conflict between his irresistible intellectual curiosity and his passionate conviction that only heavenly transcendence matters.

The rest of the "Second Anniversary" is taken up with the consideration of Heaven—the soul's company in that place, the "essential joy"
found there (a kind of joy that cannot logically exist in this life), and
the "accidental joys," which far surpass anything to be found on
earth:

> Only in Heaven joyes strength is never spent;
> And accidentall things are permanent.
> Joy of a soules arrivall ne'r decaies;
> For that soule ever joyes and ever staies.
> Joy that their last great Consummation
> Approaches in the resurrection;
> When earthly bodies more celestiall
> Shall be, then Angels were, for they could fall;
> This kinde of joy doth every day admit
> Degrees of growth, but none of losing it.
> In this fresh joy, 'tis no small part, that shee,
> Shee, in whose goodnesse, he that names degree,
> Doth injure her; ('Tis losse to be cal'd best,
> There where the stuffe is not such as the rest)
> Shee, who left such a bodie, as even shee
> Only in Heaven could learne, how it can bee
> Made better; for shee rather was two soules,
> Or like to full on both sides written Rols,
> Where eyes might reade upon the outward skin,
> As strong Records for God, as mindes within;
> Shee, who by making full perfection grow,
> Peeces a Circle, and still keepes it so,
> Long'd for, and longing for it, to heaven is gone,
> Where shee receives, and gives addition.
>   (1:265–66)

John Donne had sired twelve children, five of whom died before
reaching maturity. There is, I think, no doubt that the true subject
of the *Anniversaries* is complex and multiple—"the Idea of a Woman,
and not as she was." And yet the poet knew what loss was, and the
way in which the death of the beloved deprives the world of significance. The enormous religious and cosmological structure of his great

poems is based on the simple and terrible fact of loss. He did not need to have known Mistress Elizabeth Drury personally. Nor do we. The poems remain controversial. One recent scholar has maintained that there is a gross discrepancy between Donne's subject—seen here as essentially simple—and the extravagance of his treatment. Another has responded—sensibly, I think—that the complication of Donne's treatment is relevant to human experience, that Donne "knew that truth tends to be simple," but he also knew "that subtleties of mind, if not necessary to salvation, make life in the present world more interesting."[18]

One of the most distinguished authorities on the *Anniversaries* has observed that "these remarkable poems transform conventional praise into a symbolic mode,"[19] fusing complimentary poem, funeral elegy, sermon, hymn, and meditation into something new to European poetry. That new mode was to find imitators later in the century, most notably Marvell and Dryden. Whatever else may be stated about it, that new mode was a variety of religious poetry, and it is not surprising that the period of its composition also saw the beginnings and, to some extent, the fruition of Donne's activity as a religious poet.

Minor Poems

Much of Donne's devotional poetry was written before 1615.[20] Some of it—most of the meditative *Holy Sonnets* and "Goodfriday, 1613. Riding Westward"—belongs to his very greatest work in that mode, and consideration of these poems may conveniently be postponed for treatment in connection with the later devotional poetry. The remainder of the mid-period religious poetry is less personally intense, more occasional. *La Corona* (1608–9, also entitled "Holy Sonnets" and hence sometimes confused with the greater sequence) is a sequence of seven linked sonnets, in which the last line of each sonnet is repeated as the first line of the next, with the last line of the last sonnet repeating the first line of the first. The purpose of the form is clearly to imitate a circular crown, or "corona," to be presented as a tribute to the Deity. The poems deal with successive stages in the life of Christ: after an introductory sonnet ("Deigne at my hands this crown of prayer and praise") there are sonnets dealing with "Annunciation," "Nativitie," "Temple," "Crucifying," "Resurrection," and "Ascension."

The Litanie (1609) is the most liturgical, the least personal, of Donne's poetical works on religious subjects. It is a sequence of short lyrics, in nine-line stanzas. The first thirteen stanzas celebrate the central elements of the Christian faith, beginning with Father, Son, Holy Ghost, and Trinity, and ranging through Virgin Mary, Angels, Patriarchs, Prophets, Apostles, and Martyrs, to conclude with Confessors, Virgins, and Doctors. The remaining fifteen stanzas have the form of prayers, beseeching God to supply guidance to the faithful on earth, helping them to avoid temptation, particularly the kind of temptations resulting from spiritual extravagance or lack of moderation. The sequence constitutes an exemplary statement of the via media so prized by and so central to the Anglican temperament. The following stanza may serve to typify the sequence:

> From needing danger, to bee good,
> From owing thee yesterdaies teares to day,
> From trusting so much to thy blood,
> That in that hope, wee wound our soule away,
> From bribing thee with Almes, to excuse
> Some sinne more burdenous,
> From light affecting, in religion, newes [i.e., novelty],
> From thinking us all soule, neglecting thus
> Our mutuall duties, Lord deliver us.
>
> (1:344)

The Litanie has its share of wit, but it is, for Donne, atypically restrained. "The Crosse," on the other hand, is an extravagant example of baroque or Metaphysical excess. Despite its somber subject, the poem has a kind of irrepressible exuberance as it pursues its simple enterprise of finding the image of the cross in every aspect of experience. The speaker begins as follows: "Since Christ embrac'd the Crosse it selfe, dare I / His image, th'image of his Crosse deny?" (1:331). A few lines, from the middle and the end of the poem, will convey something of its flavor:

> Who can deny mee power, and liberty
> To stretch mine armes, and mine owne Crosse to be?
> Swimme, and at every stroake, thou art thy Crosse;
> The Mast and yard make one, where seas do tosse;
> Looke downe, thou spiest out Crosses in small things;
> Looke up, thou seest birds rais'd on crossed wings;
> All the Globes frame, and spheares, is nothing else
> But the Meridians crossing Parallels. . . .

> Be covetous of Crosses, let none fall.
> Crosse no man else, but crosse thy selfe in all.
> Then doth the crosse of Christ worke fruitfully
> Within our hearts, when wee love harmlessly
> That Crosses pictures much, and with more care
> That Crosses children, which our Crosses are.
>
> (1:332–33)

The occasional nature of the other religious poems of Donne's middle period is indicated by their titles: "Resurrection, Imperfect [i.e., unfinished]," "Upon the Annuntiation and Passion Falling upon One Day," and "Upon the Translation of the Psalmes by Sir Philip Sydney, and the Countesse of Pembroke His Sister."

Prose Works

During the period of these poetic works, Donne produced four substantial prose works of significance: *Pseudo-Martyr, Ignatius His Conclave, Essays in Divinity,* and *Biathanatos* ("a declaration of that paradox . . . that self-homicide is not so naturally a sin that it may never be otherwise"). They are of varying interest for the modern reader. *Pseudo-Martyr,* of great importance in Donne's life, and a work on which he lavished much of his intellectual power, is likely to seem impenetrable to all but the most dedicated scholars of today. Published in 1610, the *Pseudo-Martyr* is an attempt to demonstrate through argument and authority that it is altogether just and appropriate for the Roman Catholic of England to take the oath of allegiance to the ruling monarch. The subject, one may imagine, was one on which Donne had thought long and hard: years before, his own unwillingness, while still a Catholic, to take the oath of allegiance to Elizabeth I had prevented him from taking a university degree. The argumentation of the work is intricate and complicated, and the style dense; the basic point is that Catholic English, in acknowledging the monarch to be the head of the Church of England, do not compromise their own religious beliefs even though they are not themselves Anglican. The gesture is an essentially political and civil one, and to incur suffering for one's self by declining this civic obligation in the name of religious belief is to achieve what may be denominated a false martyrdom.

A word of explanation is perhaps necessary here. In modern usage the term *martyrdom* designates any death, suffering, or loss incurred as a result of a firm adherence to one's beliefs or principles. For Donne and his contemporaries, martyrdom was truly such only when suffered in the name of valid principles. In this work, as elsewhere, the opponents Donne attacks with the greatest fervor are the Jesuits, who, themselves often ardent seekers for the crown of martyrdom (one need think only of the poet Robert Southwell or Blessed Edmund Campion in Donne's own lifetime), urged their English coreligionists to do likewise. Donne, who remained sympathetic to English Catholics even after his conversion to Anglicanism, was unswervingly hostile to the Society of Jesus; some residue of guilt remaining from his Catholic upbringing and his own avoidance of martyrdom may account for some of the intensity of that hostility.[21]

Jesuits are also the butt of *Ignatius His Conclave* (1611), a high-spirited work that followed close on the heels of *Pseudo-Martyr*. It is unique in Donne's prose in being a work of fiction, although it can scarcely be said to have much of a plot. Four great innovators—Machiavelli, Paracelsus, Copernicus, and Ignatius of Loyola—die and go to Hell; the action of the work is their experiences there and the dialogues among them and their host, Satan. All four figures are of central importance not only to Donne but also to the other intellectuals of his time. Machiavelli, as is well known, had become the model for a stock figure of villainy on the Elizabethan and Jacobean stage (in Marlowe's *Jew of Malta* he even makes an appearance as Prologue)—partly because of the distortion of his views popularized by the *Contre-Machiavel* of the French Huguenot Jacques Amyot, partly because the stock figure thus created was so wonderfully viable in theatrical terms, and partly, be it admitted, because the actual thought of Machiavelli—describing political behavior in realistic terms rather than in terms of moral philosophy or Christian belief—was so deeply disturbing that its promulgator, it seemed, must be evil.

Paracelsus exerted a peculiar fascination on Donne. Although the poet refers slightingly to that worthy's medical doctrines in the "First Anniversary," Paracelsian thought is strongly present in the *Anniversaries,* as well as in such poems as the "Nocturnall upon S. *Lucies* Day," "The Extasie," and a good many others.[22] A comparable ambivalence informs Donne's attitude toward Copernicus and the other champions of the new astronomy; he nowhere indicates an unquestioning acceptance of the heliocentric hypothesis, but his imagination cannot stay away from it, constantly brooding on the possibility of its truth.

As for Ignatius, a similar ambivalence ought perhaps to be postulated: the great Spanish saint was the founder of the Society of Jesus, so firmly detested by Donne and so linked by him and other English with motifs of falsehood, deceitful ingenuity, and treason, and yet at the same time the promulgator of the techniques of formal meditation that Donne and other English Protestants, as well as Catholics, found so edifying and so worthy of adoption. However that may be, Ignatius receives short shrift in the work under consideration: at its conclusion he is seen as having a better chance than the other innovators to usurp the throne of Satan himself.

Of significance surely is the fact that innovation itself is seen as dangerous, evil, indeed infernal. In *Ignatius His Conclave,* as elsewhere, one must take note of Donne's deep-seated intellectual conservatism, curiously coexisting not only with his fascination with new ideas but also with the radical and experimental nature of his artistic techniques. In this respect, as in so many others, he stands in contrast to his younger contemporary Milton, who was as essentially conservative in his artistic stance as he was radical in his political, religious, and philosophical ideas.

The *Essayes in Divinity,* composed just before Donne's ordination but published (by his son John) for the first time only in 1651, are at the same time one of the most private and personal and one of the least revealing of the poet's prose works. In form a commentary on the opening verses of each of the first two books of the Old Testament, each of the two sections followed by a prayer, the *Essayes* give evidence of Donne's wide learning in a variety of sources, including some rather esoteric ones. It is possible that contemplation of the possibility of becoming a priest of the Church of England may have led to their composition.

Biathanatos also was not published during Donne's lifetime. Composed earlier than the other prose works discussed in this chapter (probably in 1608), it belongs to the darkest period in Donne's career, and the subject matter itself—the possibility of a moral justification for suicide—is revealing in the extreme. As one would expect, given the religious tradition of Donne's age, the work seeks to make its case not in psychological or pragmatic terms but in religious and philosophical ones. The avoidance of physical or psychological pain as a rationale for suicide does not prevent it from being sinful, but there are cases—e.g., that of Samson—in which the honor of God is served by the taking of one's life. If the honor of God, or perhaps the serving of one's fellows, is effected by self-slaughter, it may in some cases not be sinful.

A work of casuistical scholarship, *Biathanatos* is interesting to the modern reader primarily for its illumination of Donne's spiritual state during the most desperate period of his life. The author sees his dangerous melancholy not merely as a response to terribly negative circumstances but rather as a resurgence of something that has always been a part of his personality:

I have often such a sickely inclination. And whether it be, because I had my first breeding and conversation with men of a suppressed and afflicted Religion, accustomed to the despite of death, and hungry of an imagin'd Martyrdome; Or that the common Enemie find that doore worst locked against him in mee; Or because my Conscience ever assures me, that no rebellious grudging at Gods gifts, nor other sinfull concurrence accompanies these thoughts in me, or that a brave scorn, or that a faint cowardlinesse beget it, whensoever any affliction assailes me, mee thinks I have the keyes of my prison in mine owne hand, and no remedy presents it selfe so soone to my heart, as mine own sword.[23]

Both the poetry and the prose of Donne's middle period exhibit a steady intensification of the religious impulse that had always been an important part of his being. In 1615 he took orders in the Church of England. One wonders—and one will never know—if that step brought definitive rest to his inquiring and unquiet soul. One knows that it led to the creation of a very great body of religious poetry and prose.

Chapter Six
Sermons and *Devotions*

Donne is the greatest preacher of the greatest age of English pulpit oratory. Between his ordination in 1615 (with his subsequent appointment as chaplain to James I) and his death in 1631, he composed and delivered a great many sermons, some 160 of which are extant.[1] One hundred forty-five of them were printed posthumously in the folios of 1640, 1649, and 1661, an indication of the esteem in which Donne's achievement in the genre was held during his lifetime and for some generations thereafter.

The defining features of Donne's sermons are essentially the same as those of his poetry—dramatic immediacy, personal intensity, lively wit, compelling rhythms, and an extravagant use of conceited imagery (the prominence of the *concetto predicabile,* or "preachable conceit," was definitive for the sermon of the baroque age, in England as on the Continent). To some extent, the characteristics of the various sermons are influenced by the differing natures of the congregations for which they were conceived: some of the earlier sermons, delivered at the Inns of Court, and some of the sermons delivered before the king, are wittier, more obscure, more learnedly allusive, than those delivered at Saint Paul's after the poet was elevated to the post of dean in 1621. But the intensity remains constant, as does the effort to involve the congregation immediately and personally in the mysteries of salvation being expounded.

Donne's Baroque Sermons

The baroque sermon was not at attempt to elucidate the general drift of a text. Still less was it an emotional exordium loosely based on motifs found in a text. It was, rather, an "exposition erudite," a scrupulous examination of every word of the text with the aim of "applying the word to the conscience and faith of his hearers."[2] Unlike the sermons of some of the more measured and temperate of Donne's clerical contemporaries—Lancelot Andrewes, for example—Donne's are highly excitable. In the course of his examination of the text,

some detail will kindle his imagination and his emotions, and he will
launch into a passage of torrential eloquence. Such purple patches
aroused the suspicion of T. S. Eliot (who preferred Andrewes),[3] but
most modern readers find them as moving and right as the finest of
the poems.

Like his religious poems, Donne's sermons seldom if ever lay stress
on the controversial points of Christian doctrine, emphasizing rather
those items of faith on which Puritan and Anglican, Protestant and
Catholic, agree. Augustine is the theological authority most frequently cited, and certain themes—the ineffable mercy of God, the
communion of saints, human brotherhood, the power of prayer, the
desperate longing for union with God—recur obsessively. Less edifying is the obsession with death and decay and the certainty thereof,
but that emphasis is to some extent balanced by the preacher's
repeated and impassioned insistence on the doctrine of the resurrection of the body. Donne the preacher was still the man who had written "The Good-Morrow" and "The Extasie." His biographer Walton
well understood the centrality of the doctrine of resurrection in the
thought of his friend, which is why he concludes the *Life* with the
assertions that "that body which was once a temple of the Holy
Ghost" has "now become a small quantity of Christian dust" and that
he will "see it re-animated."[4]

Sermon XXIII

Donne's thematic concerns and stylistic features may be found typified as well as anywhere else in *Sermon* XXIII of the folio of 1640,
preached at Saint Paul's on Easter Day 1628. The text is a familiar
one from Paul: "For now we see through a glass darkly, but then face
to face; now I know in part, but then I shall know even as also I am
known" (1 Cor. 13:12). The preacher begins with a consideration of
the contrast between *nunc* and *tunc,* "now" and "then," and proceeds
to a consideration of the nature of sight, "the noblest of all the
senses," and of the way in which, in this life, humans have sight of
God:

For our sight of God here, our Theatre, the place where we sit and see
him, is the whole world, the whole house and frame of nature, and our *medium,* our *glasse,* is the Booke of Creatures, and our light by which we see
him, is the light of Naturall Reason. And then, for our knowledge of God

here, our Place, our Academy, our University is the Church, our *medium,* is the Ordinance of God in his Church, Preaching, and Sacraments; and our light is the light of faith. Thus we shall finde it to be, for our sight, and for our knowledge of God here. But for our sight of God in heaven, our place, our Spheare is heaven it selfe, our *medium* is the Patefaction, the Manifestation, the Revelation of God himselfe, and our light is the light of Glory. And then, for our knowledge of God there, God himself is All; God himself is the place, we see Him, in Him; God is our *medium,* we see Him, by him; God is our light; not a light which is His, but a light which is He; not a light which flowes from him, no, nor a light which is in him, but that light which is He himself. *Lighten our darknesse, we beseech thee, O Lord, O Father of lights, that in thy light we may see light,* that now we see this through thy *glasse,* thine Ordinance, and, by the good of this, hereafter *face to face.*[5]

The piling up of illustrative metaphors is fully typical of Donne's pulpit style, and the metaphor of the world as theater—already noted as a central topos of the baroque imagination—recurs throughout the sermon. Notable also is the preoccupation with seeing, a theme explored in a more learned way a few paragraphs later:

First then we consider, (before we come to our knowledge of God) our sight of God in this world, and that is, sayes our Apostle, *In speculo, we see as in a glasse.* But how doe we see in a glasse? Truly, that is not easily determined. The old Writers in the Optiques said, That when we see a thing in a glasse, we see not the thing itselfe, but a representation onely; All the later men say, we doe see the thing it selfe, but not by direct, but by reflected beames. It is a uselesse labour for the present, to reconcile them. This may well consist with both, That as that which we see in a glasse, assures us, that such a thing there is, (for we cannot see a dreame in a glasse, nor a fancy, nor a Chimera) so this sight of God, which our Apostle sayes we have *in a glasse,* is enough to assure us, that a God there is. (8:222–23)

His exploration becomes ever more extravagant and fanciful:

There is not so poore a creature but may be thy glasse to see God in. The greatest flat glasse that can be made, cannot represent anything greater then it is: If every gnat that flies were an Arch-angell, all that could but tell me, that there is a God; and the poorest worme that creepes, tells me that. If I should aske the Basilisk, how camest thou by those killing eyes, he would tell me, Thy God made me so; And if I should aske the Slow-worme, how camest thou to be without eyes, he would tell me, Thy God made me so. The Cedar is no better a glasse to see God in, then the Hyssope upon the

wall; all things that are, are equally removed from being nothing; and what-
soever hath any beeing, is by that very beeing, a glasse in which we see God,
who is the roote, and the fountaine of all beeing. The whole frame of nature
is the Theatre, the whole Volume of creatures is the glasse, and the light of
nature, reason, is our light (8:224)

Subsequently he discusses, in a more practical manner, the role of
church and Scripture in instructing the faithful in the ways of seeing
God in the glass of this world. His imagination is ignited again when
he comes to consider the direct vision of God to be vouchsafed to the
saved in the next world:

First, the Spheare, the place where we shall see him, is heaven; He that
asks me what heaven is, meanes not to heare me, but to silence me; He
knows I cannot tell him; When I meet him there, I shall be able to tell him,
and then he will be as able to tell me; yet then we shall be but able to tell
one another, This, this that we enjoy is heaven, but the tongues of Angels,
the tongues of glorified Saints, shall not be able to expresse what that heaven
is; for, even in heaven our faculties shall be finite. Heaven is not a place that
was created; for, all place that was created, shall be dissolved. God did not
plant a Paradise for himself, and remove to that, as he planted a Paradise for
Adam, and removed him to that; but God is still where he was before the
world was made. And in that place, where there are more Suns then there
are Stars in the Firmament, (for all the Saints are Suns) And more light in
another Sun, The Sun of righteousness, the Son of Glory, the Son of God,
then in all them, in that illustration, that emanation, that effusion of beams
of glory, which began not to shine 6000. yeares ago, but 6000. millions of
millions ago, had been 6000. millions of millions before that, in those eter-
nall, in those uncreated heavens, shall we see God. (8:231)

As the preacher nears the end of the sermon, the underlying preoccupation emerges in full force: the desire to be absorbed into unity
with God (one is reminded here, as in some of Donne's great hymns,
that the poet, although he seems never to have experienced a mystical
experience, deeply longed to do so). It is absolutely typical of Donne
that, when he conceives of union with God, that union is in terms of
knowledge, and that knowledge is synonymous with Love:

And so it shall be a knowledge so like his knowledge, as it shall produce
a love, like his love, and we shall love him, as he loves us. For as S. *Chrysos-
tome,* and the rest of the Fathers, whom *Oecumenius* hath compacted, interpret
it, *Cognoscam practicé, id est, accurrendo,* I shall know him, that is, imbrace

him, adhere to him. *Qualis sine fine festivitas!* what a Holy-day shall this be, which no working day shall ever follow! By knowing, and loving the unchangeable, the immutable God, *Mutabimur in immutabilitatem,* we shall be changed into an unchangeablenesse, sayes that Father, that never said anything but extraordinarily. He sayes more, *Dei praesentia si in inferno appareret,* If God could be seene, and known in hell, hell in an instant would be heaven. (8:235–236)

Sermon XXIII of the 1640 folio is typical of Donne's pulpit eloquence in its extraordinary intensity and elevation of tone, but it is also typical in that that elevation rises naturally—or so it seems—from a language that is conversational, immediate, almost, indeed, colloquial. The analogy with his lyric poetry in that respect is obvious. As a prose artist, Donne is generally classed with the Senecan, or anti-Ciceronian, movement that was so important during the first two-thirds of the seventeenth century, both in England and on the Continent. The classification is on the whole accurate, but it should be noted that whenever—one assumes—it seems appropriate or effective to the preacher he is capable of formulating a series of highly rhetorical Ciceronian periods. In his stylistic eclecticism Donne is to be classed with a great contemporaneous master of baroque prose, Sir Thomas Browne, rather than with Bacon, the great exponent of the curt style; Burton, the great exponent of the loose style; or such minor enthusiasts of Senecanism as Owen Felltham or John Earle.[6]

Other Sermons

Some of Donne's major preoccupations as sermon writer may be suggested by a smattering of passages—perhaps "purple"—from a number of his works in that genre: the following, for example, from XXII of the 1640 folio, typifies quite adequately the fierce preoccupation with death:

When I consider what I was in my parents loynes (a substance unworthy of a word, unworthy of a thought) when I consider what I am now, (a Volume of diseases bound up together, a dry cynder, if I look for naturall, for radicall moisture, and yet a Spunge, a bottle of overflowing Rheumes, if I consider accidentall; an aged childe, a gray-headed Infant, and but the ghost of mine own youth) When I consider what I shall be at last, by the hand of death, in my grave, (first, but Putrifaction, and then, not so much as putrifaction, I shall not be able to send forth so much as an ill ayre, not any ayre

at all, but shall be all insipid, tastelesse, savourlesse dust; for a while, all
wormes, and after a while, not so much as wormes, sordid, senslesse, name-
lesse dust) When I consider the past, and present, and future state of this
body, in this world, I am able to conceive, able to expresse the worst that
can befall it in nature, and the worst that can be inflicted upon it by man,
or fortune; But the least degree of glory that God hath prepared for that
body in heaven, I am not able to expresse, not able to conceive. (8:390)

The last sentence hints at the compensatory vision that is equally
a part of the Donne of the *Sermons*. A brief passage from XIV of the
1649 folio does much the same thing:

Here a bullet will aske a man, where's your arme; and a Wolf wil ask a
woman, where's your breast? A sentence in the Star-chamber will aske him,
where's your ear, and a months close prison will aske him, where's your
flesh? a fever will aske him, where's your Red, and a morphew will aske him,
where's your white? But when after all this, when *after my skinne worms shall
destroy my body, I shall see God,* I shall see him in my flesh, which shall be
mine as inseparably, (in the *effect,* though not in the *manner*) as the *Hypostati-
call union* of God, and man, in Christ, makes our nature and the Godhead
one person in him. My flesh shall no more be none of mine, then Christ shall
not be man, as well as God. (3:113)

The same sermon expatiates further on the theme of the sight of
God, stressing in Donne's typical manner that it will ultimately be a
vision *in the flesh:*

I shall see him, *In carne suâ, in his flesh:* And this was one branch in *Saint
Augustines* great wish, That he might have seen Rome in her state, That he
might have heard S. *Paul* preach, That he might have seen Christ in the
flesh: *Saint Augustine* hath seen Christ in the flesh one thousand two hundred
yeares; in Christs glorifyed flesh; but, it is with the eyes of his understanding, and in his soul. Our flesh, even in the Resurrection, cannot be a specta-
cle, a perspective glasse to our soul. We shall see the Humanity of Christ
with our bodily eyes, then glorifyed; but, that flesh, though glorifyed, cannot make us see God better, nor clearer, then the soul alone hath done, all
the time, from our death, to our resurrection. But as an indulgent Father,
or as a tender mother, when they go to see the King in any Solemnity, or
any other thing of observation, and curiosity, delights to carry their child,
which is flesh of their flesh, and bone of their bone, with them, and though
the child cannot comprehend it as well as they, they are as glad that the
child sees it, as that they see it themselves; such a gladnesse shall my soul
have, that this flesh, (which she will no longer call her prison, nor her

tempter, but her friend, her companion, her wife) that this flesh, that is, I, in the re-union, and redintegration of both parts, shall see God; for then, one principall clause in her rejoycing, and acclamation, shall be, that this flesh is her flesh; *In carne mêa, in my flesh I shall see God.* (3:112)

He admits that the vision of God in the soul is sufficient, but the joy he takes in the idea of the vision in the flesh is fully manifest.

This passage illustrates the preacher's point with a metaphor involving the figure of the king. In another of Donne's sermons, the funerary oration that Donne delivered over the remains of his benefactor and friend, a specific king is evoked—James I, the deceased. A passage from it may be quoted to illustrate Donne's use of compelling rhythms and lexical repetitions to achieve an emotional and dramatic effect. The recurrence, in what follows, of the word *dead* recalls the practice of the poet as well as of the prose artist, imitating, to press into service another of Donne's favorite metaphors, the tolling of a bell:

And when you shall find that hand that had signed to one of you a *Patent* for *Title,* to another for *Pension,* to another for *Pardon,* to another for *Dispensation, Dead:* That hand that settled Possessions by his *Seale,* in the *Keeper,* and rectified *Honours* by the *sword,* in his *Marshall,* and distributed relief to the *Poore,* in his *Almoner,* and *Health* to the *Diseased,* by his *immediate Touch,* Dead: That Hand that ballanced his *own three Kingdomes* so equally, as that none of them complained of one another, nor of him, and carried the *keyes* of all the Christian World, and locked up, and let out *Armies* in their due season, Dead; how poore, how faint, how pale, how momentany, how transitory, how empty, how frivolous, how Dead things, must you necessarily thinke *Titles,* and *Possessions,* and *Favours,* and all, when you see that Hand, which was the *hand of Destinie,* of *Christian Destinie,* of the *Almighty God,* lie dead? It was not so *hard* a hand when we touched it last, nor so *cold* a hand when we kissed it last: That hand which was wont *to wipe all teares from all our eyes,* doth now but presse and squeeze us as so many spunges, filled one with one, another with another cause of teares. (6:290)

The echoes of the refrain of the "First Anniversary" remind us again of the underlying consistency of Donne's work.

The passage from the sermon on James illustrates, among other things, Donne's awareness of what a well-deployed Ciceronian period can accomplish in the way of creating suspense and tension. The following peroration, from XXVI of the 1640 folio, evokes terror rather than pity, and does so most effectively:

That that God should loose and frustrate all his owne purposes and prac-
tises upon me, and leave me, and cast me away, as though I had cost him
nothing, that this God at last, should let this soule goe away, as a smoake,
as a vapour, as a bubble, and that then this soule cannot be a smoake, nor
a vapour, nor a bubble, but must lie in darknesse, as long as the Lord of
light is light it selfe, and never a sparke of that light reach to my soule;
What Tophet is not Paradise, what Brimstone is not Amber, what gnashing
is not a comfort, what gnawing of the worme is not a tickling, what torment
is not a marriage bed to this damnation, to be secluded eternally, eternally,
eternally from the sight of God? (5:267)

Devotions upon Emergent Occasions

The *Sermons* are by definition public works, whatever the degrees of
personal intensity and even idiosyncrasy Donne weaves into them to
achieve the desired effects. More centrally personal, more private
even, are the *Devotions upon Emergent Occasions,* his other prose masterpiece. Inspired by a serious illness of 1623, the *Devotions* consists of
twenty-three sections, each divided into a "Meditation," an "Expostulation," and a "Prayer." As the tripartite structure suggests, the *Devotions* exemplifies the practice of formal meditation, that form of
spiritual and psychological exercise formulated in the mid-sixteenth
century by Ignatius of Loyola and, as noted, of enormous influence on
baroque religious writers, Protestant as well as Catholic.[7]

In the *Devotions,* the Ignatian "composition of place" (here called
simply "Meditation") corresponds to a phase in the speaker's illness
as he traces it from its onset through its course to its crisis and finally
to the beginning of its cure. The "Expostulation" examines and ana-
lyzes the spiritual significance of the scene composed, and the
"Prayer" constitutes the Ignatian "colloquy" in which the Deity is addressed with passionate immediacy. The relationship of the three
parts of each section is in no sense rigidly mechanical; each part flows
into the next, and the direct address to God typically begins in the
Expostulation, to be carried on into the Prayer.

Part 1 bears the title "Insultus Morbi Primus; The first alteration,
The first grudging of the sicknesse," and the opening sentences of its
meditation serve to illustrate the nervous intensity, the colloquial immediacy, of the entire work:

Variable, and therefore miserable condition of Man; this minute I was well,
and am ill, this minute. I am surpriz'd with a sodaine change, and alteration

to worse, and can impute it to no cause, nor call it by any name. We study *Health*, and we deliberate upon our *meats*, and *drink*, and *ayre*, and *exercises*, and we hew, and wee polish every stone, that goes to that building; and so our *Health* is a long and a regular work; But in a minute a Canon batters all, overthrowes all, demolishes all; a *Sicknes* unprevented for all our diligence, unsuspected for all our curiositie; nay, undeserved, if we consider only *disorder*, summons us, possesses us, destroyes us in an instant.[8]

The sentences have a characteristic Senecan flavor, their members seemingly arranged in a haphazard and capricious manner, but in fact artistically crafted to create an effect of spontaneity. For all the air of casual afterthought, the whole meditation is put together with care—as the rhetorically powerful reprise of opening motifs in the last sentence of the meditation will perhaps suggest to some readers: "O perplex'd discomposition, O ridling distemper, O miserable condition of Man!" (310).

In no other of Donne's works—not even in the *Anniversaries*—is the thematic opposition more marked between the traditional, universally symbolic view of the world and the emergent, deeply problematic vision of the world adumbrated by the new astronomy. The underlying structure is symbolic in the traditional sense—each stage of the physical illness corresponds not only to the operation of sin on the spiritual level but also to the manifestations of disorder on the cosmic level (induced, of course, by sin). But that underlying symbolism is rendered dubious by the alternative world views available and adduced. The meditation of the fourth *Devotion* begins with an evocation of the traditional linkage of microcosm and macrocosm that is virtually classical:

It is too little to call *Man* a *little World;* Except *God*, Man is a *diminutive* to nothing. Man consists of more pieces, more parts, than the world; than the world doeth, nay than the world is. And if those pieces were extended, and stretched out in Man, as they are in the world, Man would bee the *Gyant*, and the Worlde the *Dwarfe*, the World but the *Map*, and the Man the *World*. If all the *Veines* in our bodies, were extended to *Rivers*, and all the *Sinewes*, to *Vaines of Mines*, and all the *Muscles*, that lye upon one another, to *Hilles*, and all the *Bones* to *Quarries* of stones, and all the other pieces, to the proportion of those which correspond to them in the world, the *Aire* would be too little for this *Orbe* of Man to move in, the firmament would bee but enough for this *Starre;* for, as the whole world hath nothing, to which something in man doth not answere, so hath man many pieces, of which the whole world hath no representation. (312–13)

However deeply marred by original sin, the world conceived in the traditional view—hierarchical, symbolic, comprehensible—was comforting not only in its assurance of cosmic order but also in its consistent assertion of humanity's blighted grandeur. The frequency of Donne's evocations of the traditional view, in the *Devotions* as in the *Anniversaries,* is perhaps a reflex of the author's awareness of the powerful challenges to it presented by the new philosophy. In the *Devotions* he refers several times to the new ideas about the cosmos, mentioning, for example, the idea of the plurality of inhabited worlds (315–16) and, humorously, his feverish dizziness as an argument for the Copernican hypothesis (353–54). As in the *Anniversaries,* the flaw in the orderly system is related to human sinfulness. The meditation of the tenth *Devotion* opens as follows: "This is *Natures nest of Boxes;* The Heavens containe the *Earth,* the *Earth, Cities, Cities, Man.* And all these are *Concentrique;* the common *center* to them all, is decay" (324).

John Donne, dean of Saint Paul's, had not forgotten the theaters he had frequented in his passionate youth. The *Devotions* are saturated with allusions to the plays of Marlowe and Shakespeare: in the meditation in *Devotion* VI he writes as follows: "A man that is not afraid of a *Lion* is afraid of a *Cat;* not afraid of *starving,* and yet is afraid of some *joynt of meat* at the table . . . not afraid of the sound of *Drummes,* and *Trumpets,* and *Shot* . . . and is afraid of some particular *harmonious instrument*" (317). There is here probably a reminiscence of Shylock in *The Merchant of Venice:*

> Some men there are love not a gaping pig,
> Some that are mad if they behold a cat,
> And others when the bagpipe sings i' the nose
> Cannot contain their urine.
>
> (4.1.47–50)

In the meditation in VIII, in a discussion of the common human frailty shared even by kings, we read these lines: "A glasse is not the lesse brittle, because a *Kings* face is represented in it; nor a King the lesse brittle, because God is represented in him." (320). The reference is surely to Richard's abdication speech in *Richard II,* when he gazes into the mirror: "A brittle glory shineth in this face— / As brittle as the glory is the face" (4.1.287–88). And in a famous passage on self-

destruction in the meditation in XII we encounter allusions to both
the suicide of Bajazet in Marlowe's *Tamburlaine* and that of Portia in
Julius Caesar:

There are too many *Examples* of men, that have bin their own *executioners,* and
that have made hard shift to bee so; some have alwayes had *poyson* about
them, in a *hollow ring* upon their finger, and some in their *Pen* that they used
to write with: some have beat out their *braines* at the wal of their prison, and
some have eate the *fire* out of their chimneys: and one is said to have come
neerer our case than so, to have strangled himself, though his hands were
bound, by crushing his throat between his knees; But I doe nothing upon
my selfe, and yet am mine owne *Executioner.* (329–30)

The central theme of the *Devotions upon Emergent Occasions* is human
sinfulness, as symbolized by proneness to physical disease, and the ne-
cessity of divine grace. Of the many minor themes that thread their
way throughout the work, none is more important than the theme of
brotherhood, adumbrated in the meditation on solitude in *Devotion* V:

As *Sicknes* is the greatest misery, so the greatest misery of sicknes, is *solitude;*
when the infectiousnes of the disease deterrs them who should assist, from
comming; even the *Phisician* dares scarse come. *Solitude* is a torment which
is not threatned in *hell* it selfe. . . . *God* himselfe would admit a *figure of
Society,* as there is a plurality of persons in *God,* though there bee but one
God; and all his externall actions testifie a love of *Societie,* and *communion.* In
Heaven there are *Orders of Angels,* and *Armies of Martyrs,* and *in that house,
many mansions;* in *Earth, Families, Cities, Churches, Colleges,* all *plurall things;*
and lest either of these should not be company enough alone, there is an
association of both, a *Communion of Saints,* which makes the *Militant,* and
Triumphant Church, one Parish; So that *Christ,* was not out of his *Dioces,* when
hee was upon the *Earth,* nor out of his *Temple,* when he was in our flesh.
(314–15)

More concrete, immediate, and poignant as a treatment of the theme
is the passage that concludes the meditation of *Devotion* VII:

How many are sicker (perchance) than I, and laid on their wofull straw at
home (if that corner be a home) and have no more hope of helpe, though
they die, than of preferment, though they live? Nor doe no more expect to
see a *phisician* then, than to be an *Officer* after; of whome, the first that takes
knowledge, is the *Sexten* that buries them; who buries them in *oblivion* too?

for they doe but fill up the number of the dead in the Bill [i.e., the weekly list of deaths from the Plague], but we shall never heare their *Names,* till wee reade them in the Booke of life, with our owne. How many are sicker (perchance) than I, and thrown into *Hospitals,* where (as a fish left upon the Sand, must stay the tide) they must stay the *Phisicians* houre of visiting, and then can bee but *visited?* How many are sicker (perchaunce) than all we, and have not this *Hospitall* to cover them, not this straw, to lie in, to die in, but have their *Grave-stone* under them, and breathe out their soules in the eares, and in the eies of passengers, harder than their bed, the flint of the street? That taste of no part of our *Phisick,* but a *sparing dyet;* to whom ordinary porridge would bee *Julip* enough, the refuse of our servants, *Bezar* enough, and the off-scouring of our Kitchen tables, *Cordiall* enough. O my *soule,* when thou art not enough awake, to blesse thy *God* enough for his plentifull mercy, in affoording thee many *Helpers,* remember how many lacke them, and helpe them to them, or to those other things, which they lacke as much as them. (319–20)

These passages and similar ones (for Donne, even the fact that his physicians consult, join themselves together as professionals, becomes a "figure of society") serve as a background and preparation for the great sequence of *Devotions* on the tolling bell (XVI, XVII, XVIII) that constitutes at once the crisis of the protagonist's illness and the climax of the work. In the meditation of *Devotion* XV, subtitled "Interea insomnes noctes Ego duco, Diesque. I sleepe not day or night," the protagonist contemplates the familiar analogy between sleep and death, regretting that he is compelled to confront death in its terrible aspect rather than under the comforting metaphor. As he continues, presumably, in his sleepless state, he hears (in *Devotion* XVI) from a nearby church the daily tolling of the bell for the funerals of the dead; he identifies himself imaginatively with his fellow human beings who have died: "Here the *Bells* can scarse solemnise the funerall of any person, but that I knew him, or knew that he was my *Neighbour:* we dwelt in houses neere to one another before, but now hee is gone into that house, into which I must follow him" (336).

The meditation of *Devotion* XVII—"Nunc lento sonitu dicunt, Morieris. Now, this Bell tolling softly for another, saies to me, Thou must die"—carries the identification to a mighty climax that is surely the most famous passage in all of Donne's prose:

Perchance hee for whom this *Bell* tolls, may be so ill, as that he knowes not it tolls for him; and perchance I may thinke my selfe so much better than I am, as that they who are about mee, and see my state, may have caused it to toll for mee, and I knowe not that. The *Church* is *Catholike*, universall, so are all her *Actions; All* that she does, belongs to *all*. When she *baptizes a child*, that action concernes mee; for that child is thereby connected to that *Head* which is my *Head* too, and engraffed into that *body*, whereof I am a *member*. And when she *buries a Man*, that action concernes me: All *mankinde* is of one *Author*, and is one *volume*; when one Man dies, one *Chapter* is not *torne* out of the *booke*, but *translated* into a better *language*; and every *Chapter* must be so *translated*; God emploies several *translators*; some peeces are trans-lated by *age*, some by *sicknesse*, some by *warre*, some by *justice*; but *Gods* hand is in every translation; and his hand shall binde up all our scattered leaves againe, for that *Librarie* where every *booke* shall lie open to one another. . . . The *Bell* doth toll for him that *thinkes* it doth; and though it *intermit* againe, yet from that *minute* that that occasion wrought upon him, hee is united to God. . . . Who bends not his *eare* to any *bell*, which upon any occasion rings? but who can remove it from that *bell*, which is passing a peece of *him-selfe* out of this world? No man is an *Iland*, intire of it selfe; every man is a peece of the *Continent*, a part of the *maine*; if a *Clod* bee washed away by the *Sea, Europe* is the lesse, as well as if a *Promontorie* were, as well as if a *Mannor* of thy friends or of *thine owne* were; any mans *death* diminishes *me*, because I am involved in *Mankinde; And* therefore never send to know for whom the *bell* tolls; It tolls for *thee.* (338–39)

Devotion XVIII effects the complete imaginative identification— "At inde Mortuus es, Sonitu celeri, pulsuque agitato. The Bell rings out, and tells me in him, that I am dead"—and the protagonist, hav-ing undergone a symbolic death, is able to undergo spiritual rebirth, and experiences the slow return to physical health that is the sub-stance of the last *Devotions,* XIX, XX, XXI, XXII, and XXIII. The work concludes with the doctors' warning to the protagonist of "the fearefull danger of relapsing," a warning that is, of course, to be taken spiritually as well as materially.

The serious illness that evoked the *Devotions upon Emergent Occasions* probably gave rise as well to Donne's "Hymne to God the Father," and some scholars[9] believe that the great "Hymne to God My God, in My Sicknesse" was written at around the same time, despite the tradition, going back to Walton, that holds that the latter was writ-ten on the poet's deathbed. Whatever the truth of the matter, the concerns of the *Devotions* are very much those of the later devotional poetry, and to Donne's religious poetry as a whole we now turn.

Chapter Seven
Divine Poems

Much of Donne's religious poetry—including some of his finest—was written during the decade preceding his ordination in 1615. The best-known of his religious poems are, no doubt, his *Holy Sonnets*—not the sequence of seven sonnets subtitled "La Corona," but the other group of nineteen sonnets appearing under that title in Grierson's edition. In the first edition of Donne's poems (posthumous, 1633), twelve sonnets make up this latter group; the 1635 edition added four more, and three additional ones were added from manuscript in the later nineteenth century. Grierson printed all nineteen as one continuous sequence, and scholarship in the earlier part of our century agreed in dating this sequence to the years after not only Donne's ordination but also the death of his wife.

More recent scholarship—specifically that of Helen Gardner—has radically corrected our understanding in this matter. Gardner has demonstrated that the nineteen sonnets fall into three groups, the first two of which are purposefully coherent: (1) a meditative sequence of twelve sonnets (those of the 1633 edition), composed probably in 1609, the first six treating the themes of death and judgment, the last six that of divine love; (2) a meditative sequence of four sonnets (those added in the 1635 edition), penitential in character and composed between 1609 and 1611, (3) the three unrelated sonnets found in the Westmoreland manuscript and not published until the nineteenth century, composed some time after 1617.[1]

Holy Sonnets and Holy Meditation

As my use of the term *meditative* indicates, the *Holy Sonnets* are in part the product of the practice of formal meditation—a point established definitively by both Gardner and Martz.[2] More precisely, the typical holy sonnet assumes the form of the third stage of the meditation, the colloquy—as if an entire process of meditation had crystallized and assumed metrical form. One might consider, for example, #1 (second sequence) in Gardner's numbering (#1 in Grierson's)[3]:

> Thou hast made me, And shall thy worke decay?
> Repaire me now, for now mine end doth haste,
> I runne to death, and death meets me as fast,
> And all my pleasures are like yesterday;
> I dare not move my dimme eyes any way,
> Despaire behind, and death before doth cast
> Such terrour, and my feeble flesh doth waste
> By sinne in it, which it t'wards hell doth weigh;
> Onely thou art above, and when towards thee
> By thy leave I can looke, I rise againe;
> But our old subtle foe so tempteth me,
> That not one houre my selfe I can sustaine;
> Thy Grace may wing me to prevent his art,
> And thou like Adamant draw mine iron heart.
>
> (1:322)

This sonnet is typical of Donne's work in the genre not only in its quality as a meditative colloquy, but also for its tone of desperation. The *Holy Sonnets* are, to be blunt about it, not edifying from an orthodox Christian point of view (as are, for example, the devotional poems of George Herbert—not only for the Anglican but for any Christian, whether Protestant or Catholic). There is little hope in Donne's *Holy Sonnets,* and not very much trust. What one encounters, rather, is naked fear: the speaker desperately wishes to go to Heaven and—even more markedly—to escape Hell. The concentration on the self is extreme, and the terrified eloquence of that self, unforgettable.

The speaker in these poems lavishes upon God all the ingenuity and eloquence he had once devised for his earthly mistresses. The following poem, for example (#1 of first sequence in Gardner; #2 in Grierson), has the rigorously argumentative structure that practically defines not only Donne's lyric poetry but, indeed, Metaphysical poetry as a whole:

> As due by many titles I resigne
> My selfe to thee, O God, first I was made
> By thee, and for thee, and when I was decay'd
> Thy blood bought that, the which before was thine;
> I am thy sonne, made with thy selfe to shine,
> Thy servant, whose paines thou hast still repaid,
> Thy sheepe, thine Image, and, till I betray'd
> My selfe, a temple of thy Spirit divine;
> Why doth the devill then usurpe on mee?

Why doth he steale, nay ravish that's thy right?
Except thou rise and for thine owne worke fight,
Oh I shall soone despaire, when I doe see
That thou lov'st mankind well, yet wilt'not chuse me,
And Satan hates mee, yet is loth to lose mee.

(1:322)

Donne's Style

The *Holy Sonnets* have a great deal in common with the amorous
Songs and Sonets, apart from intellectual flavor and argumentative
structure. There is also, for example, the relentlessly dramatic, immediate, and colloquial quality, well-illustrated in the following (#3 of
first sequence in Gardner; #6 in Grierson):

This is my playes last scene, here heavens appoint
My pilgrimages last mile; and my race
Idly, yet quickly runne, hath this last pace,
My spans last inch, my minutes latest point,
And gluttonous death, will instantly unjoynt
My body, and soule, and I shall sleepe a space,
But my'ever-waking part shall see that face,
Whose feare already shakes my every joynt:
Then, as my soule, to'heaven her first seate, takes flight,
And earth-borne body, in the earth shall dwell,
So, fall my sinnes, that all may have their right,
To where they'are bred, and would presse me, to hell.
Impute me righteous, thus purg'd of evill,
For thus I leave the world, the flesh, the devill.

(1:324)

The irregular, yet inescapable recurrence of the word *last,* with its
variant *latest,* anticipates the technique Donne was to employ later as
preacher, and the ubiquitous baroque topos of the theater occurs to
intensify the macabre effect.

Conceit and paradox are deployed in the *Holy Sonnets* with a lavish-
ness unmatched even in the amorous lyrics. In "Oh my blacke Soule!
now thou art summoned" (#2 of first sequence in Gardner; #4 in
Grierson), the elaborate metaphors identifying the sinful soul with an
exiled traitor and then with a condemned thief are followed by a blaze
of self-contradictory imagery, in which the color red assumes three

different symbolic valences and then operates in a manner that contradicts normal experience:

> Oh my blacke Soule! now thou art summoned
> By sicknesse, deaths herald, and champion;
> Thou art like a pilgrimm, which abroad hath done
> Treason, and durst not turne to whence hee is fled,
> Or like a thiefe, which till deaths doome be read,
> Wisheth himself delivered from prison;
> But damn'd and hal'd to execution,
> Wisheth that still he might be imprisoned.
> Yet grace, if thou repent, thou canst not lacke;
> But who shall give thee that grace to beginne?
> Oh make thy selfe with holy mourning blacke,
> And red with blushing, as thou art with sinne;
> Or wash thee in Christs blood, which hath this might
> That being red, it dyes red soules to white.
>
> (1:323)

Similar operations are to be observed in "I am a little world made cunningly" (#2 of second sequence in Gardner; #5 in Grierson), in which the physical properties of the elements of fire and water turn out to be both multiple and self-contradictory:

> I am a little world made cunningly
> Of Elements, and an Angelike spright,
> But black sinne hath betraid to endlesse night
> My worlds both parts, and (oh) both parts must die.
> You which beyond that heaven which was most high
> Have found new sphears, and of new lands can write,
> Powre new seas in mine eyes, that so I might
> Drowne my world with my weeping earnestly,
> Or wash it, if it must be drown'd no more:
> But oh it must be burnt! alas the fire
> Of lust and envie have burnt it heretofore,
> And made it fouler; Let their flames retire,
> And burne me ô Lord, with a fiery zeale
> Of thee and thy house, which doth in eating heale.
>
> (1:324)

The poem is rather more hopeful than the majority of the *Holy Sonnets,* in that respect bearing a certain affinity to the very well-known sonnet "Death be not proud" (#6 of the first sequence in Gardner; #10 in Grierson).

Sexual imagery is obsessive in the *Holy Sonnets* (as religious imagery is in the amorous lyrics), and such imagery concentrates with formidable power the dramatic, passionate, and paradoxical elements that virtually define Donne's achievement in the genre of the devotional lyric. The relationship between the amorous poems and the *Holy Sonnets* is sometimes overt, as in #3 of second sequence in Gardner; #3 in Grierson:

> O Might those sighes and teares returne againe
> Into my breast and eyes, which I have spent,
> That I might in this holy discontent
> Mourne with some fruit, as I have mourn'd in vaine;
> In mine Idolatry what showres of raine
> Mine eyes did waste? what griefs my heart did rent?
> That sufferance was my sinne; now I repent;
> 'Cause I did suffer I must suffer paine.
> Th'hydroptique drunkard, and night-scouting thiefe,
> The itchy Lecher, and selfe tickling proud
> Have the remembrance of past joyes, for reliefe
> Of comming ills. To (poore) me is allow'd
> No ease; for, long, yet vehement griefe hath beene
> Th'effect and cause, the punishment and sinne.
>
> (1:323)

In #9 of the first sequence in Gardner; #13 in Grierson, the speaker meditates on the image of Christ crucified and on the divine love that motivated the sacrifice. The aim of the poem is to achieve for the speaker assurance that he will be forgiven and saved, and in the sestet of the sonnet he addresses Christ in a kind of blasphemous parody of the line he had used to employ with his mistresses: the sense of the lines, in effect, is: "O come; show pity—only the ugly ones are hardhearted":

> No, no; but as in my idolatrie
> I said to all my profane mistresses,
> Beauty, of pitty, foulnesse onely is
> A signe of rigour: so I say to thee,
> To wicked spirits are horrid shapes assign'd,
> This beauteous forme assures a pitious
> minde.
>
> (1:328)

One of the most celebrated of the *Holy Sonnets* (#10 of first sequence in Gardner; #14 in Grierson) combines the features of these poems in an unforgettable manner. The first quatrain urges the triune God (employing the imperative mode dominant in the entire sequence) to force the speaker, as it were, into salvation. The metaphor is the homely one of a tinker or similar workman repairing a battered pot, and in lines 2, 3, and 4 the collocation of three verbs with one emblematizes the mystery of the Trinity:

> Batter my heart, three person'd God; for, you
> As yet but knocke, breathe, shine, and seeke to mend;
> That I may rise, and stand, o'erthrow mee,' and bend
> Your force, to breake, blowe, burn and make me new.
> (1:328)

The metaphor shifts radically in the second quatrain, which presents a miniature allegory in which the soul is likened to a town occupied by enemy forces (the Devil), struggling to admit the besieging army (God), but frustrated by the weakness or treason of the municipal authorities (his own reason):

> I, like an usurpt towne, to'another due,
> Labour to'admit you, but Oh, to no end,
> Reason your viceroy in mee, mee should defend,
> But is captiv'd, and proves weake or untrue.
> (1:328)

Force and violence are the qualities that bestow unity of tone on the poem—the violence of physical labor in the first quatrain, the violence of warfare in the second. In the sestet of the sonnet it becomes sexual violence, rape:

> Yet dearely' I love you, 'and would be loved faine,
> But am betroth'd unto your enemie:
> Divorce mee, 'untie, or breake that knot againe,
> Take mee to you, imprison mee, for I
> Except you'enthrall mee, never shall be free,
> Nor ever chast, except you ravish mee.
> (1:328)

The dazzling paradoxes of the conclusion reaffirm the degree to which
Donne was an artist of the baroque—not only in his reckless extravagance of technique but also in his deep conviction that, in a world
where all is illusion, divine truth inevitably presents itself in terms
that seem absurd or self-contradictory to earthly wisdoms. A similar
theme is apparent at the end of one of the Westmoreland sonnets (#2
of Westmoreland in Gardner; #18 in Grierson), a poem that reveals
that, even after his ordination, Donne was in some doubt whether the
true Church was Rome, Canterbury, or Geneva:

> Show me deare Christ, thy spouse, so bright and clear.
> What! is it She, which on the other shore
> Goes richly painted? or which rob'd and tore
> Laments and mournes in Germany and here?
> Sleepes she a thousand, then peepes up one yeare?
> Is she selfe truth and errs? now new, now outwore?
> Doth she, and did she, and shall she evermore
> On one, on seaven, or on no hill appeare?
> Dwells she with us, or like adventuring knights
> First travaile we to seeke and then make Love?
> Betray kind husband thy spouse to our sights,
> And let myne amorous soule court thy mild Dove,
> Who is most trew, and pleasing to thee, then
> When she'is embrac'd and open to most men.
>
> (1:330)

The sonnet concludes with the paradox that Christ, the bridegroom
of the Church, is pleased when His bride is sexually possessed by as
many men as possible. He thus becomes a *wittold,* or cooperative
cuckold—to the Renaissance mind (or to *earthly* conceptions) the most
contemptible of beings.

Another of the Westmoreland sonnets (#1 of Westmoreland in
Gardner; #17 in Grierson) is also personal and private in a very special sense. Its subject is the death of Donne's wife, and in it the poet
reveals that he cannot resign himself to her loss, that, despite the
consolations of Christian Platonism, he cannot satisfy himself with
the love of God alone. It is a deeply moving poem:

> Since she whom I lov'd hath payd her last debt
> To Nature, and to hers, and my good is dead,
> And her Soule early into heaven ravished,

Wholly on heavenly things my mind is sett.
Here the admyring her my mind did whett
To seeke thee God; so streames do shew their head;
But though I have found thee, and thou my thirst hast fed,
A holy thirsty dropsy melts mee yett.
But why should I begg more Love, when as thou
Dost wooe my soule for hers; offring all thine:
And dost not only feare least I allow
My Love to Saints and Angels things divine,
But in thy tender jealosy dost doubt
Least the World, Fleshe, yea Devill putt thee out.

(1:330)

"Goodfriday, 1613. Riding Westward"

Apart from the two meditative sequences of *Holy Sonnets,* the most important of Donne's preordination religious poems is "Goodfriday, 1613. Riding Westward." In intellectual form a complete meditation, the poem begins with a "composition by similitude"[4] in which the speaker considers the disturbing symbolic significance of the situation in which he finds himself: although it is Good Friday, he is riding toward the west, thus turning his back on Palestine, where Christ's sacrifice was accomplished (as elsewhere in Donne, *west* also carries connotations of death—a further source of distress):

Let mans Soule be a Spheare, and then, in this,
The intelligence that moves, devotion is,
And as the other Spheares, by being growne
Subject to forraigne motions, lose their owne,
And being by others hurried every day,
Scarce in a yeare their naturall forme obey:
Pleasure or businesse, so, our Soules admit
For their first mover, and are whirld by it.
Hence is't, that I am carryed towards the West
This day, when my Soules forme bends toward the East.

(1:336)

The analysis that constitutes the second movement of the poem is a blaze of paradox, pun, and conceit as the speaker considers the overwhelming implications of the Passion:

> There I should see a Sunne, by rising set,
> And by that setting endlesse day beget;
> But that Christ on this Crosse, did rise and fall,
> Sinne had eternally benighted all.
> Yet dare I'almost be glad, I do not see
> That spectacle of too much weight for mee.
> Who sees Gods face, that is selfe life, must dye;
> What a death were it then to see God dye? . . .
> Could I behold those hands which span the Poles,
> And tune all spheares at once, peirc'd with those holes?
> Could I behold that endlesse height which is
> Zenith to us, and our Antipodes,
> Humbled below us? or that blood which is
> The seat of all our Soules, if not of his,
> Made durt of dust, or that flesh which was worne
> By God, for his apparell, rag'd, and torne?
>
> (1:336–37)

In the colloquy that concludes the meditation, the speaker addresses the crucified Christ and asserts that he has turned his back on him that he may be scourged by the Deity and thus purged of his sins. Thus, through wit, the speaker create a symbolism more comforting and affirmative than that with which the poem began:

> Though these things, as I ride, be from mine eye,
> They'are present yet unto my memory,
> For that looks towards them; and thou look'st towards mee,
> O Saviour, as thou hang'st upon the tree;
> I turne my backe to thee, but to receive
> Corrections, till thy mercies bid thee leave.
> O thinke mee worth thine anger, punish mee,
> Burne off my rusts, and my deformity,
> Restore thine Image, so much, by thy grace,
> That thou may'st know mee, and I'll turne my face.
>
> (1:337)

The three great *Hymnes* of Donne's later years have a quality of assurance, even a serenity, that are very unlike the tone of many of the *Holy Sonnets*. The earliest of them, "A Hymne to Christ, at the Authors Last Going into Germany," was occasioned by the poet's trip to Germany in May 1619 as chaplain to Lord Doncaster on one of the latter's diplomatic missions. As in "Goodfriday, 1613," Donne seeks the symbolic significance of the details that make up the voyage:

> In what torne ship soever I embarke,
> That ship shall be my embleme of thy Arke;
> What sea soever swallow mee, that flood
> Shall be to mee an embleme of thy blood;
> Though thou with clouds of anger do disguise
> Thy face; yet through that maske I know those eyes,
>> Which, though they turne away sometimes
>> They never will despise.
>
> (1:352)

In the second stanza the speaker attempts to free himself from all earthly attachments in order to be able to dedicate himself to God exclusively. But, as the third stanza indicates, he has trouble doing so, and he urges God to liberate him by force from earthly loves. There are obvious connections to the sonnet "Batter my heart, three person'd God," and even closer connections to "Since she whom I lov'd hath payd her last debt" (the latter poem may have been composed at around the same time as the "Hymne to Christ"):

> I sacrifice this Iland unto thee,
> And all whom I lov'd there, and who lov'd mee;
> When I have put our seas twixt them and mee,
> Put thou thy sea betwixt my sinnes and thee.
> As the trees sap doth seeke the root below
> In winter, in my winter now I goe,
>> Where none but thee, th'Eternall root
>> Of true Love I may know.
>
> Nor thou nor thy religion dost controule,
> The amorousnesse of an harmonious Soule,
> But thou would'st have that love thy selfe; As thou
> Art jealous, Lord, so I am jealous now,
> Thou lov'st not, till from loving more, thou free
> My soule: Who ever gives, takes libertie:
>> O, if thou car'st not whom I love
>> Alas, thou lov'st not mee.
>
> (1:353)

The poem concludes with an expressed desire to enter a kind of darkness of total deprivation, in which the speaker may concentrate his entire being on the experience of God:

> Seale then this bill of my Divorce to All,
> On whom those fainter beames of love did fall;
> Marry those loves, which in youth scattered bee
> On Fame, Wit, Hopes (false mistresses) to thee.
> Churches are best for Prayer, that have least light:
> To see God only, I goe out of sight:
>   And to scape stormy dayes, I chuse
>   An Everlasting night.
>
>   (1:353)

The imagery is that of traditional mysticism, particularly that associated with the motif of the "negative way." But Donne's temperament is very unlike that of such mystical poets as Crashaw or Vaughan, still more unlike that of San Juan de la Cruz. One suspects that the "Hymne to Christ" is a poem *about* the mystical experience rather than one expressing such an experience; one suspects that, though he would very much have liked to, Donne never had a mystical experience—something that surely exists, whether one's own beliefs incline one to regard it as the result of divine grace or as the result of abnormal psychology.

The Final Hymns

"A Hymne to God the Father," composed after Donne's grave illness of 1623, is something of a technical tour de force, its eighteen lines being built on only two rhymes. It is typical of a great deal of baroque religious poetry in that it is playful, abounding in puns and other phenomena of wit, and in that its playfulness in no way cancels out its sincere and purposeful seriousness. The playful and the serious are not, to the baroque mind, opposed terms. The pun on *sonne* as at once the celestial orb and the son of God is a familiar one in seventeenth-century texts, and centuries of Donne commentary have noted the pun on the poet's name which occurs in the refrain line concluding each of the poem's three stanzas. Scholarship has been less willing to consider the possibility of another pun—on *more* and Ann More, the poet's late wife. We cannot, however, dismiss the possibility out of hand: both the "Hymne to Christ" and the Westmoreland sonnet clearly indicate that Donne found his unquenchable love for the lost Ann to be an obstacle to his own achieving a state of complete devotion to God, and such a state was, undoubtedly, the aim of his later years:

"A Hymne to God the Father"

I.

Wilt thou forgive that sinne where I begunne,
Which was my sin, though it were done before?
Wilt thou forgive that sinne; through which I runne,
And do run still: though still I do deplore?
When thou hast done, thou hast not done,
For, I have more.

II.

Wilt thou forgive that sinne which I have wonne
Others to sinne? and, made my sinne their doore?
Wilt thou forgive that sinne which I did shunne
A yeare, or two: but wallowed in, a score?
When thou hast done, thou hast not done,
For I have more.

III.

I have a sinne of feare, that when I have spunne
My last thred, I shall perish on the shore;
But sweare by thy selfe, that at my death thy sonne
Shall shine as he shines now, and heretofore;
And, having done that, Thou haste done,
I feare no more.

(1:369)

Whether composed after the 1623 illness or indeed on the poet's deathbed, the "Hymne to God My God, in My Sicknesse" is an appropriate work with which to conclude a consideration of Donne's achievement as a devotional poet. The themes, motifs, and techniques that had dominated his life's work—conceited imagery, radical paradox, a preoccupation with geography and cartography, dramatic tone, colloquial diction, the desperate desire for transcendence—are brought together to form a consummate masterpiece of baroque devotional poetry:

"Hymne to God My God, in My Sicknesse"

Since I am comming to that Holy roome,
   Where, with thy Quire of Saints for evermore,
I shall be made thy Musique; As I come
   I tune the Instrument here at the dore,
And what I must doe then, thinke here before.

Whilst my Physitians by their love are growne
   Cosmographers, and I their Mapp, who lie
Flat on this bed, that by them may be showne
   That this is my South-west discoverie
Per fretum febris, by these streights to die,

I joy, that in these straights, I see my West;
   For, though theire currants yeeld returne to none,
What shall my West hurt me? As West and East
   In all flatt Maps (and I am one) are one,
So death doth touch the Resurrection.

Is the Pacifique Sea my home? Or are
   The Easterne riches? Is *Ierusalem?*
Anyan, and *Magellan,* and *Gibraltare,*
   All streights, and none but streights, are wayes to them,
Whether where *Iaphet* dwelt, or *Cham,* or *Sem.*

We thinke that *Paradise* and *Calvarie,*
   Christs Crosse, and *Adams* tree, stood in one place;
Looke Lord, and finde both *Adams* met in me;
   As the first *Adams* sweat surrounds my face,
May the last *Adams* blood my soule embrace.

So, in his purple wrapp'd receive mee Lord,
   By these his thornes give me his other Crowne;
And as to others soules I preach'd thy word,
   Be this my Text, my Sermon to mine owne,
   Therfore that he may raise the Lord throws down.

                          (1:368–69)

Chapter Eight
Reputation and Influence

Donne's literary works enjoyed great popularity and received great admiration during his lifetime and for a good generation after his death. His reputation, of course, is not to be conceived in terms of a mass audience—there was none in seventeenth-century England (except, perhaps, in the London theater). His contemporaneous reputation existed among the privileged classes, the wits, the "understanders" addressed in the anonymous preface to the first, posthumous edition of his poems. In his lifetime the poet published only the *Anniversaries,* the "Elegie on Prince Henry," and the poem on Thomas Coryat's *Crudities,* in addition to several prose works. His reputation as a poet, confined to an elite, was based on widely circulated manuscripts and miscellanea and on poems recorded in commonplace books.

His reputation as a prose writer was, similarly, restricted to an intellectual elite, but it was the definitive elite of Jacobean and Caroline England. His *Sermons* were greatly admired during his lifetime and frequently published during the succeeding generation. Such works as the *Pseudo-Martyr* and the *Devotions upon Emergent Occasions* attracted the attention of the privileged and powerful—including Kings James I and Charles I.

The "School of Donne"

His influence, also, began early and proved significant. Although it is demonstrably erroneous to speak—as so many enthusiasts from 1920 to 1960, and even later, have—of a "School of Donne" that includes George Herbert, Richard Crashaw, Andrew Marvell, and Henry Vaughan (the great religious poets of the Metaphysical movement)—there was a true "School of Donne." It began with Edward, Lord Herbert of Cherbury, and Henry King, and it included, in Donne's own time, such poets as Thomas Carew and, in the next generation, Cowley, Suckling, Lovelace, and Cleveland. The great Metaphysical poets of England, after Donne, do not show any conspicuous or systematic imitation of him: George Herbert was more influenced

by Sidney than by Donne; Crashaw was inspired by Herbert but more
strongly influenced by such Continental models as Marino; Vaughan
was influenced significantly by Donne in his secular poetry but far
more significantly by George Herbert in his religious poetry; and the
great and sophisticated eclectic Marvell, although he utilized Donne,
used Jonson and others more consistently. The major Metaphysicals
would have written much as they did had Donne never existed: their
style is a version of the great international baroque style, which had
announced itself in England even before Donne in the work of Robert
Southwell, William Alabaster, and, to some extent, Sir Philip
Sidney.[1]

The true "School of Donne" begins with Herbert of Cherbury, a
faithful imitator, and Henry King, an occasionally inspired disciple.
It continues with the Cavalier poets, most of whom show an allegiance divided between Donne and Ben Jonson—his friend, rival, and
sometimes hostile critic. Some of Jonson's dicta—that he "esteem[ed]
John Done the first poet in the world in some things," but that
"Done himself, for not being understood, would perish," and that
"Done, for not keeping of accent, deserved hanging"[2]—have helped
give plausibility to the myth that English poets of the earlier seventeenth century may be neatly divided into followers of Donne and
Jonson. The Cavaliers themselves—conventionally regarded as Jon-
sonians—knew better. Thomas Carew, the most self-conscious and
sophisticated artist among them, knew how to praise both Jonson and
Donne with equal acumen, and his "Elegie upon the Death of the
Deane of Pauls, Dr. John Donne" is the first truly perceptive and important piece of criticism of the poet and preacher:

> The Muses garden with Pedantique weedes
> O'rspred, was purg'd by thee; the lazie seeds
> Of servile imitation throwne away;
> And fresh invention planted, Thou didst pay
> The debts of our penurious bankrupt age;
> Licentious thefts, that make poetique rage
> A Mimique fury, when our soules must bee
> Possest, or with Anacreons Extasie,
> Or Pindars, not their owne; The subtle cheat
> Of slie Exchanges, and the jugling feat
> Of two-edg'd words, or whatsoever wrong
> By ours was done the Greeke, or Latine tongue,
> Thou hast redeem'd, and open'd Us a Mine

Of rich and pregnant phansie, drawne a line
Of masculine expression, which had good
Old Orpheus seene, Or all the ancient Brood
Our superstitious fooles admire, and hold
Their lead more precious, then thy burnish't Gold,
Thou hadst beene their Exchequer, and no more
They each in others dust, had rak'd for Ore. . .

. . .

But thou art gone, and thy strict lawes wiil be
Too hard for Libertines in Poetrie.
They will repeale the goodly exil'd traine
Of gods and goddesses, which in thy just raigne
Were banish'd nobler Poems, now, with these
The silenc'd tales o'th'Metamorphoses
Shall stuffe their lines, and swell the windy Page,
Till Verse refin'd by thee, in this last Age
Turne ballad rime. . .

. . .

Let others carve the rest, it shall suffice
I on thy Tombe this Epitaph incise.
Here lies a King, that rul'd as hee thought fit
The universall Monarchy of wit;
Here lie two Flamens, and both those, the best,
Apollo's first, at last, the true Gods Priest.[3]

In his own lesser way Carew applied effectively in his own poems the lessons he had learned from Donne: colloquial ease, dramatic immediacy, natural diction, and brilliantly witty metaphor are the hallmarks of his art, and these features manifest themselves also in the poems of Suckling and Lovelace—in combination with shorter, more chiseled lines modeled after Jonson's. A decade or so later, in the work of Cowley and Cleveland, the traits that reflect Donne's influence have become so automatic and so exaggerated as to be annoying, and in the 1660s—in the work of, of all people, the young John Dryden—those same traits have become clearly decadent.

Donne and Neoclassicism

It was the mature Dryden who was to sum up—though in a judicious and measured manner not matched by some later neoclassicists—the reaction against Donne and against baroque style in general. Esteeming Donne as "the greatest Wit, though not the best

Poet of our Nation,"[4] Dryden censures him for his lack of decorum,
particularly in the famous passage in which he observes that Donne
"affects the metaphysics, not only in his satires, but in his amorous
verses, where nature only should reign; and perplexes the minds of
the fair sex with nice speculations of philosophy, when he should engage their hearts, and entertain them with the softnesses of love."[5]
Recurrent in Dryden's critical work is the praise of Edmund Waller
and Sir John Denham for the smoothness and "correctness" of their
versification, and implicit in such praise is the disapproval of Donne's
"roughness."

A comparably ambiguous attitude toward Donne manifests itself in
the work of Alexander Pope, who did his predecessor the honor of
subjecting his satires to metrical paraphrase but, at the same time,
showed condescension by making those paraphrases more "correct"—
both metrically and lexically. Still, both Dryden and Pope recognized
the greatness of Donne as intellect and artist. Their lesser contemporaries were in the process of forgetting him altogether, or, if they re-
membered him, ranking him rather lower than Cowley.

It was in Samuel Johnson's "Life of Cowley" in his *Lives of the English Poets* (1779) that the term *Metaphysical poets* and the conception
of Donne as the father of that race were given a currency and an acceptance that were to continue until the early years of the present century. Justly concentrating on the distinctive nature of the radical
Metaphysical conceit, Dr. Johnson writes, in a famous passage, that
"the most heterogeneous ideas are yoked by violence together,"[6] but,
to his neoclassical mind, this reliance on wit led to "unnaturalness,"
and such unnaturalness, together with Donne's metrical "harshness,"
calls the quality of his poetic gift into question.

Like Dryden and Pope, however, Johnson has a mixed attitude toward Donne and his fellows. "To write on their plan," he concedes,
"it was at least necessary to read and think."[7] Dryden, Pope, and
Johnson were all literary intellectuals of the highest order, and, despite the rigidities of their neoclassical orthodoxy, they were compelled to recognize some merit in Donne's literary achievement. Their
contemporaries, the common readers of the eighteenth century, by
and large forgot Donne altogether as a poet. His reputation as a great
preacher remained, but the outmoded extravagance of baroque pulpit
style inspired little real admiration. Joseph Warton and Richard
Hurd were among the few other eighteenth-century literary figures
who showed some limited appreciation of Donne as poet.[8]

Donne in the Nineteenth Century

As is common knowledge, the romantics reacted strongly against their neoclassical predecessors. The reaction did not, however, effect a favorable reassessment of Donne and other baroque poets—possibly because, although the romantics conceived of "Nature" in ways radically different from the Augustans, they continued to hold convictions that construed the baroque manner as artificial, and hence vicious. There are a few great exceptions, most notably Coleridge and De Quincey, both of whom admired Donne, and for the right reason—the quality of his imagination. In their critical observations, in Charles Lamb's, and, to a certain extent, in some ambiguous pronouncements in Hazlitt and Landor, we find the beginnings of a shift in critical attitudes toward Donne that was, from around 1830 until the end of the nineteenth century, to make itself slowly but ever more steadily apparent.[9]

Donne's prose shared in the revaluation of his poetry, and its acceptance in the course of the nineteenth century was more rapid and marked. Coleridge, and even Wordsworth, admired his sermons, and the Victorians, somewhat later, embraced them with fervor. Popular—and especially academic—opinion continued to reject the poetry when it did not ignore it. But Robert Browning admired Donne's poetry sincerely, and—in his own cultivation of dramatic and conversational elements—clearly was influenced by it. In America Emerson, Thoreau, and, especially, James Russell Lowell counted among his champions. By the turn of the century the stage was set for a major reestimate of Donne's importance, and it came with a vengeance.

The Twentieth Century

This study began with a passing reference to the young and ill-fated golden lad Rupert Brooke. Brooke's enthusiasm for Donne, and for such other Jacobean figures as John Webster, was not an individual eccentricity but rather a manifestation of a shift of sensibility that was quite generally apparent in the opening years of our century. Its most important monument was Grierson's great 1912 edition of the *Poetical Works* of John Donne, and it is from that year and that edition that one may date the transformation of Donne from a kind of dubious *Randfigur* in the canon of English poets to one of its central and most stable names.

From the 1920s through the 1940s and into the 1950s, in both Britain and America, Donne enjoyed a position of special privilege. Familiarity with, and a taste for, his poetry and prose came to be seen, in both academic and nonacademic literary circles, as the mark of a superior sensibility, and the features of his style were exalted over those of the English romantics (especially Shelley) and even over those of Milton. For the first time since the seventeenth century his work came to exert a profound and wide influence on the compositions of contemporary poets; seen in the works of writers as diverse as T. S. Eliot, John Crowe Ransom, W. H. Auden, and Theodore Roethke.

The major document in the mid-century vogue of Donne was Eliot's very influential 1921 essay "The Metaphysical Poets."[10] Eliot argues that Donne and the other Metaphysical poets possess a capacity for synthesizing into artistic unity the disparate elements of experience: they "feel their thought as immediately as the odor of a rose."[11] He goes on to posit a "dissociation of sensibility," which set in during the later seventeenth century to the great disadvantage of poetry. This formulation has something of the shape of myth, and the sweeping historical generalization fails to hold up if we examine it critically, but it caught the fancy of a whole generation and had a powerful effect not only on the reading of poetry in the twenties, thirties, and forties, but also on its writing. Of particular significance was the justification it provided for conceited imagery like Donne's— precisely the element of technique most roundly condemned by Dr. Johnson and all the others who had accused Donne of "unnaturalness." Ernest Hemingway's best-selling 1940 novel *For Whom the Bell Tolls,* taking its title and its epigraph from Donne's *Devotions,* served to make the poet and preacher's name famous to a public wider than that of the academy and the little magazine.

Donne's occasional pose of cynicism and his frankness in sexual matters no doubt recommended him to a generation disillusioned by the bloodshed and hypocrisy of World War I and by the Great Depression, a generation also influenced by Freud and by the revolt against the repressive sexual mores of the nineteenth century. But a simple historical explanation along such lines is in no sense satisfactory. The strong revival of interest in Donne antedated World War I, and the "high modernism" that was the dominant artistic style between 1920 and 1950 had its origins in the decade before the outbreak of the Great War: one need think only of Picasso and Braque, of Stravinsky, Schönberg, and the later Mahler, of Apollinaire, Pound and the Vortex group, Eliot's early poetry, Italian futurism, and German expressionist painting and poetry.

Artists of high modernism felt a consistent sympathy with the attitudes, values, and stylistic features of the baroque, and the rehabilitation of Donne and the other English Metaphysical poets is best seen as an aspect of a general and distinctly international rediscovery of baroque art—parallel to the German rediscovery of their baroque literature, to the Spanish rehabilitation of the reputations of Góngora and Calderón, to the French discovery of poets they had almost forgotten (like Théophile de Viau) or entirely forgotten (like Jean de Sponde or Jean de la Ceppède). Perhaps the intellectuals of the time, rejecting such nineteenth-century norms as realism, sincerity, and "nature," found in the frank artificiality and frequent playfulness of baroque art something to rejoice in rather than condemn, something to use as a model rather than as a bad example. In their enthusiasm they were often narrow and unfair—as in their rejection of Milton and Shelley—but they brought back into literary life some values that had been slighted for more than two centuries.

Conclusion

The age (1920–50) that privileged Donne was distinguished by a combination of formalism and eccentricity—in poetry and fiction, in painting and music, in popular culture (e.g., jazz), in literary theory and criticism. Formalist criticism (which, in the Anglo-American world went under the name *New Criticism*) has been much misrepresented in recent years. Far from seeking a dogmatic and exclusive interpretation of a text, the New Critics characteristically sought a multiplicity of meanings; their favorite catch-phrases, after all, were *tension, paradox, ambiguity,* and *ambivalence.* The charge that they tended to cut the text off from its human context in biography and history is, though exaggerated, rather more justified. The mode of being of Donne's poetry and prose—dramatic, artificial, highly wrought, playful and serious at the same time—lent itself superbly to the New Critical conception of the text as artifact, and a very high proportion of the great bulk of critical writing devoted to Donne during those decades has the form of "explication." There were exceptions, of course, as in the contributions of historically oriented critics such as Louis I. Bredvold, Merritt Y. Hughes, Nicolson, and Martz (or, on the European continent, Legouis, Mario Praz, and Arno Esch).

But, on the whole, the extraformal dimension of Donne's achievement was slighted.

The artistic and intellectual orthodoxies and fashions of the period just under discussion did not survive the decade of the 1950s—a decade that introduced abstract expressionism, aleatoric music, happenings, beat poetry, confessional poetry, projective verse, and rock music, or that of the 1960s, with the sexual revolution, the drug culture, and computers. On the level of theoretical and critical discourse, there appeared a newly conceived and more sophisticated myth criticism (e.g., Northrop Frye) and structuralism. The spontaneous, the nonintellectual and even the anti-intellectual, and the instinctive were given a new validation, and a particular text, far from being isolated for special scrutiny, was to be stirred into the general stew.

Art and thought are almost always predictive. What were, in the 1950s, fashions in art and criticism became, in the 1960s, manners, morals, and life-style. Under the impetus of political awareness, beatniks became hippies. After 1960 it was evident that a new cultural period had arrived, one very different from the period 1920–50. In the seventies and eighties structuralism was followed by poststructuralism, deconstructionism, and other critical movements. During this period—that of present writing—what has happened to the reading and study of John Donne, and what have been the vicissitudes of his reputation?

One may begin by noting that Donne's work is no longer central to contemporary literature and to thinking about literature. In the high modernist/formalist period, Donne's poetry and prose epitomized, at least in the Anglo-American world, what literature was or should be. Poetry written during that period often showed his influence; literary theory was, at least to some extent, based on his practice; and the skill with which one analyzed a Donne poem was considered evidence of one's abilities as a practical critic. All that has changed. Most contemporary poetic voices mimic other models, and most recent literary theory has taken a path that has led it into thickets of philosophical and/or linguistic speculation in which the possibility of a poetics based on actual literary practice is but dimly seen, if at all. As for practical criticism, current fashion favors the performing of sophisticated and fantastic operations upon a previously innocent, or unviolated, text. Such criticism cannot be interested in a body of texts that, like Donne's, perform their own sophisticated and fantastic operations very nicely by themselves, thank you, with no need of interference from a creative critic. The cynically inclined might see the difference as being between "Look what this text is doing" (formalist practice) and "Look what I'm doing to this text" (some current practice).

The foregoing remarks have reference to the most novel and original developments of the past thirty years. Needless to say, more traditional and conventional research and criticism continue to be carried out, on Donne as on other literary figures. He continues to receive a good deal of scholarly attention (as Milton and Shelley did, even at the height of the high modernist period), and immensely important contributions to our knowledge of Donne have been made in recent years by Barbara Kiefer Lewalski, Joan Webber, Arnold Stein, Rosalie L. Colie, and others.

Given the whirligig of taste, one might have expected that postmodernist criticism would denigrate Donne as modernist criticism had denigrated Shelley, but this has not happened. One of the welcome developments in literary theory and criticism since 1960 has been the rehabilitation of Shelley and the other English romantics, and a remarkable clarification of our understanding of them. But no devaluation of Donne's reputation has occurred, no dislodging of him from the position in the canon of English literature won for him in the early part of the twentieth century. He occupies a secure place in school, college, and university curricula; paperbound volumes of his poems and even his prose works are readily available in all good bookstores; citations from his writings have passed into the everyday speech of cultivated people. He continues to be recognized as a great lyric poet (probably the greatest love poet of the English language), as the greatest English preacher, and as a towering figure of the baroque age. It is very unlikely—as long as there are people who are interested in literature—that John Donne will be removed from his appropriate position in the first rank of English poets and prose writers.

Notes and References

Chapter One

1. John Donne, *Poetical Works,* ed. H. J. C. Grierson, 2 vols. (1912; reprint ed., Oxford: Oxford University Press, 1953).
2. T. S. Eliot, "The Metaphysical Poets," in *Selected Essays* (New York: Harcourt, Brace, 1950).
3. Merritt Y. Hughes, "Kidnapping Donne," *University of California Publications in English* 4 (1934):61–89.
4. Mary Paton Ramsey, *Les Doctrines médiévales chez Donne* (London: Oxford University Press, 1917); Michael F. Moloney, *John Donne: His Flight from Medievalism* (Urbana: University of Illinois Press, 1944); Hiram Haydn, *The Counter-Renaissance* (New York: Grove Press, 1950); Kathleen Raine, "John Donne and the Baroque Doubt," *Horizon* 11 (1945):371–95; Wylie Sypher, *Four Stages of Renaissance Style* (Garden City, N.Y.: Doubleday & Co., 1955); William Empson, "Donne the Space Man," *Kenyon Review* 19 (1957):337–99.
5. Marjorie Hope Nicolson, *The Breaking of the Circle* (Evanston, Ill.: Northwestern University Press, 1950); Louis I. Bredvold, "The Naturalism of Donne in Relation to Some Renaissance Traditions," *JEGP* 22 (1923):471–502; Louis L. Martz, *The Poetry of Meditation,* rev. ed. (New Haven, Conn.: Yale University Press, 1962).
6. Donald L. Guss, *John Donne, Petrarchist* (Detroit: Wayne State University Press, 1966).
7. See John Donne, *The Divine Poems,* ed. Helen Gardner (1952; reprint ed., Oxford: Clarendon Press, 1959), xxxviii–1; Martz, 211–19; R. C. Bald, *John Donne,* ed. Wesley Milgate (New York and Oxford: Oxford University Press, 1970), 76–77.
8. In the Preface to *Pseudo-Martyr.* See Bald, *Donne,* 67.
9. Sir Richard Baker, *Chronicle of the Kings of England* (1643), quoted in Bald, *Donne,* 72.
10. Bald, *Donne,* 50–52.
11. *Poetical Works,* ed. Grierson, 1:33, 53.
12. The term is J. B. Leishman's, in *The Monarch of Wit* (London: Hutchinson University Library, 1951), 149–50.
13. Bredvold, "Naturalism of Donne."
14. This interpretation is contested by Helen Gardner, "The 'Metempsychosis' of John Donne," *TLS,* 29 December 1972, 1587–88.
15. *Divine Poems,* ed. Gardner, xxxviii–1.

16. The definitive edition is *The Sermons of John Donne,* ed. George R. Potter and Evelyn M. Simpson, 10 vols. (1953–62; reprint ed., Berkeley and Los Angeles: University of California Press, 1984).

17. Izaak Walton, "Life of Dr. John Donne," in *Seventeenth-Century Prose and Poetry,* ed. A. Witherspoon and F. J. Warnke, 2d ed. (New York: Harcourt, Brace & World, 1963), 263.

18. Ibid. 265; *Divine Poems,* ed. Gardner, xxxiv.

19. Louis L. Martz, *The Poem of the Mind* (New York and Oxford: Oxford University Press, 1966), 5–7.

20. F. J. Warnke, *Versions of Baroque* (New Haven, Conn.: Yale University Press, 1972), 69–70.

21. Quoted in Bald, *Donne,* 7.

22. Walton, "Life of Donne," 27.

Chapter Two

1. See Heinrich Wöfflin, *Renaissance und Barock* (Munich: T. Ackermann, 1888), 82–85.

2. Cf. Warnke, *Versions of Baroque,* 12–13, and passim.

3. Ibid., 10–12.

4. See, respectively: Nicolson, *The Breaking of the Circle,* rev. ed. (New York: Columbia University Press, 1960); Martz, *The Poetry of Meditation;* Joseph Anthony Mazzeo, *Renaissance and Seventeenth-Century Studies* (New York: Columbia University Press, 1964); and Lowry Nelson, Jr., *Baroque Lyric Poetry* (New Haven, Conn.: Yale University Press, 1961).

5. F. J. Warnke, "Baroque Once More: Notes on a Literary Period," *New Literary History* 1, no. 2 (Winter 1970):145–62.

6. See E. R. Curtius, *European Literature and the Latin Middle Ages,* trans. W. R. Trask (New York: Pantheon, 1953).

7. *Poetical Works,* ed. Grierson, 1:237. Further citations from this edition will be in the text.

8. In *Seventeenth-Century Prose and Poetry,* ed. Witherspoon and Warnke, 69.

9. F. J. Warnke, ed., *European Metaphysical Poetry* (New Haven, Conn.: Yale University Press, 1961), 63–66.

10. The poem is "The Baite," which parodies "Come live with me and be my love."

11. These last features are noted as early as Donne's contemporary Thomas Carew, in his "Elegy upon the Death . . . of Dr. John Donne."

12. *Seventeenth-Century Prose and Poetry,* ed. Witherspoon and Warnke, 103.

13. Ibid., 65.

Chapter Three

1. Bald, *Donne,* 200.

2. John Donne, *Poetry and Prose,* ed. F. J. Warnke (New York: Random House, 1967), 300.

3. See Alvin B. Kernan, *The Cankered Muse* (New Haven, Conn.: Yale University Press, 1959), passim for a discussion of this false etymology and its effects.

4. *Poetical Works,* ed. Grierson, 2:219.

5. See J. E. Spingarn, ed., *Critical Essays of the Seventeenth Century,* 3 vols. (1907; reprint ed., Bloomington: Indiana University Press, 1957), 1:xxix.

6. Thomas Hobbes, "Answer to Davenant's Preface before *Gondibert,*" in *Critical Essays,* ed. Spingarn, 2:59.

7. *Poetical Works,* ed. Grierson, 2:130–33.

8. *John Donne: The Elegies and The Songs and Sonnets,* ed. Helen Gardner (Oxford: Clarendon Press, 1965), xxxi–xlvi.

9. Andrew Marvell, *Poems and Letters,* ed. H. M. Margoliouth, 2d. ed. 2 vols., (Oxford: Oxford University Press, 1952), 1:48.

10. *Elegies and Songs and Sonnets,* ed. Gardner, xxxi.

Chapter Four

1. The position is ably defended by Theodore Redpath in *The Songs and Sonets of John Donne,* ed. Redpath (London: Methuen, 1956), xv–xvi.

2. Edmund Spenser, *Poetical Works,* ed. J. C. Smith and E. de Selin-court (Oxford: Oxford University Press, 1970), 568.

3. Clay Hunt, *Donne's Poetry* (New Haven, Conn.: Yale University Press, 1954), 55–57.

4. For a definitive exposition of this tradition, see Nicolson, *Breaking of the Circle* (1960).

5. Actually, the very earliest application of the term *metaphysical* is to be credited not to Dryden but to William Drummond, Laird of Hawthornden (1585–1649), who observed in a letter to a friend that "some Men of late (Transformers of every Thing) have consulted upon her [poetry's] Reformation, and endeavoured to abstract her to *Metaphysical* ideas, and *Scholastical* Quiddities, denuding her of her own Habits, and those Ornaments with which she hath amused the whole World some Thousand Years." (Quoted in R. Wallerstein, *Studies in Seventeenth-Century Poetic* [Madison: University of Wisconsin Press, 1950], 26.)

In his *Discourse concerning the Original and Progress of Satire* (1693), Dryden remarked that Donne "affects the metaphysics, not only in his satires, but in his amorous verses, where nature only should reign; and perplexes the minds of the fair sex with nice speculations of philosophy, when he should engage their hearts, and entertain them with the softnesses of love" (*Essays of John Dryden*, ed. W. P. Ker, 2 vols. [Oxford: Oxford University Press, 1900] 2:19). This is the background to Dr. Johnson's famous characterization, in his *Lives of the English Poets* (1779–81) of "a race of writers that may be termed the *metaphysical poets*" (Samuel Johnson, *Lives of the English Poets*, 2 vols. [London: Dent, 1925], 1:11–12).

6. Arnold Stein, *John Donne's Lyrics* (Minneapolis: University of Minnesota Press, 1962), 102–4.

7. This discussion is based on my analysis of the poem in *Poetry and Prose*, ed. Warnke, xvii–xx.

8. Stein, *Donne's Lyrics*, 158.

9. F. J. Warnke, "Donne's 'The Anniversarie,' " *Explicator* 16, no. 2 (November 1957):11–12.

10. Walton, "Life of Donne," 257.

11. *Poetical Works*, ed. Grierson, 2:10.

12. Leishman, *The Monarch of Wit*, rev. ed. (London: Hillary, 1962), 175–76, 202. Martz, *Poetry of Meditation* (New Haven, Conn.: Yale University Press, 1954), 214–15. John Shawcross, "Donne's 'A Nocturnall Upon S. Lucies Day,' " *Explicator*, 23, item 56 (1965).

13. Martz, *Poetry of Meditation*, 215.

14. Torquato Tasso, *Gerusalemme liberata*, ed. A. M. Carini (Milan: Feltrinelli, 1961), 6.

15. Helen Gardner, *The Business of Criticism* (Oxford: Oxford University Press, 1959), 52–75.

16. *Poetical Works*, ed. Grierson, 2:xlvi–xlvii; Pierre Legouis, *Donne the Craftsman* (Paris: Henri Didier, 1928), 68–69. N. J. C. Andreasen, *John Donne: Conservative Revolutionary* (Princeton: Princeton University Press, 1967), 168–78.

17. See George Williamson, "The Convention of 'The Extasie,' " in *Seventeenth Century Contexts* (London: Faber & Faber, 1960), 63–77.

18. For a treatment of this convention see Warnke, *Versions of Baroque*, 104–13.

19. See *Elegies and Songs and Sonnets*, ed. Gardner, 185.

20. Helen Gardner, "The Argument about 'The Extasie,' " in *Elizabethan and Jacobean Studies* (Oxford: Oxford University Press, 1959), 279–306, maintains that the lines are not primarily a persuasion to physical love. Andreasen, *John Donne*, argues the moralistic view. See also Pierre Legouis, *Donne the Craftsman* (Paris: Henri Didier, 1928), 61–69.

21. E. M. W. Tillyard, "A Note on Donne's *Extasie*," *Review of English Studies* 19 (1943):67–70.

22. Leishman, *Monarch of Wit* (1951), 52–53.

Chapter Five

1. Quoted in Bald, *Donne,* 138–39.
2. Ibid., 9.
3. *Songs and Sonets,* ed. Redpath, 139–40
4. Lord Herbert of Cherbury, *Poems,* ed. G. C. Moore Smith (Oxford: Clarendon Press, 1923), 9–13.
5. D. A. Keister, "Donne and Herbert of Cherbury: an Exchange of Verses," *PMLA* 8 (1947):430–34.
6. Bald, *Donne,* 269.
7. *John Donne: The Anniversaries,* ed. Frank Manley (Baltimore: Johns Hopkins University Press, 1963), 1–2.
8. Ibid., 4.
9. Ibid., 7.
10. John Donne, *Poetical Works,* ed. H. J. C. Grierson (Oxford: Oxford University Press, 1971), xxxviii.
11. *The Anniversaries,* ed. Manley, 14.
12. Martz, *Poetry of Meditation* (1954), 221.
13. Nicolson, *Breaking of the Circle* (1960), 81–82.
14. Ibid., 102–4.
15. *The Anniversaries,* ed. Manley, 20–40.
16. Martz, *Poetry of Meditation* (1954), 13–20, and passim.
17. See, for example, Barbara Kiefer Lewalski, *Donne's "Anniversaries" and the Poetry of Praise* (Princeton: Princeton University Press, 1973), 3 ff., 273 ff., and passim.
18. John Carey, *John Donne* (London and New York: Oxford University Press, 1981), 101–3; Thomas Willard, "Donne's Anatomy Lesson: Vesalian or Paracelsian?" *John Donne Journal* 3, no. 1 (1984):35–57, esp. 56.
19. Lewalski, *Donne's "Anniversaries,"* 4–5.
20. See above, Chap. 1, 10.
21. Carey, *John Donne,* 15–36, and passim, stresses particularly the theory that Donne's Catholic upbringing left on him a permanent mark.
22. See Mazzeo, *Renaissance and Seventeenth-Century Studies,* 60–89, and Willard, "Donne's Anatomy Lesson."
23. Quoted in Bald, *Donne,* 231.

Chapter Six

1. The standard edition is *The Sermons of John Donne,* ed. Potter and Simpson.
2. *Poetical Works,* (Oxford, 1971), ed. Grierson, xliii.
3. T. S. Eliot, "Lancelot Andrewes," in *Selected Essays,* 302.
4. Walton, "Life of Donne," 271.

5. *Sermons,* ed. Potter and Simpson, 8:220–21. Subsequent citations follow in the text.

6. See Joan Webber, *Contrary Music* (Madison: University of Wisconsin Press, 1963).

7. See Martz, *Poetry of Meditation* (1954).

8. *Poetry and Prose,* ed. Warnke, 308–9. Further references to this edition follow in the text.

9. *Divine Poems,* ed. Gardner, 132–35.

Chapter Seven

1. *Divine Poems,* ed. Gardner, v.

2. Ibid., xxix–xxxv; Martz, *Poetry of Meditation* (1954).

3. In citing the *Holy Sonnets* I shall give the numberings provided by both Gardner and Grierson.

4. Martz, *Poetry of Meditation* (1954), 54–56.

Chapter Eight

1. See Martz, *Poem of the Mind,* 33–53.

2. Ben Jonson, "Conversations with William Drummond of Hawthornden," *Literary Criticism of Seventeenth-Century England,* ed. E. W. Taylor (New York: Knopf, 1967), 85, 87, 84.

3. M. K. Starkman, ed., *Seventeenth-Century English Poetry,* 2 vols. (New York: Knopf, 1967), 116–18.

4. John Dryden, *Poems and Fables,* ed. J. Kinsley (London: Oxford University Press, 1962), 467 (in his Preface to "Eleonora").

5. Dryden, *Essays,* ed. Ker, 2:19.

6. Samuel Johnson, "Life of Cowley," in *Lives of the English Poets,* 1:11–12.

7. Ibid., 1:14.

8. Raoul Granquist, *The Reputation of John Donne, 1779–1873* (Uppsala, Sweden: Almquist & Wiksell, 1975), 22–24.

9. Ibid., 72–110.

10. T. S. Eliot, "Metaphysical Poets," 241–50.

11. Ibid., 247.

Selected Bibliography

PRIMARY SOURCES

Poetical Works. Edited by H. J. C. Grierson. 2 vols. 1912. Reprint. Oxford: Oxford University Press, 1953. One-volume paperback edition, 1971.

Complete English Poems. Edited by C. A. Patrides. London: Everyman, 1985.

John Donne: The Anniversaries. Edited with an introduction and commentary by Frank Manley. Baltimore: Johns Hopkins University Press, 1963.

The Divine Poems. Edited with an introduction and commentary by Helen Gardner. 1952. Reprint. Oxford: Clarendon Press, 1959.

John Donne: The Elegies and the Songs and Sonnets. Edited with an introduction by Helen Gardner. Oxford: Clarendon Press, 1965.

The Epithalamions, Anniversaries, and Epicedes. Edited with an introduction and commentary by Wesley Milgate. Oxford: Clarendon Press, 1978.

John Donne: The Satires, Epigrams and Verse Letters. Edited with an introduction and commentary by W. Milgate. Oxford: Clarendon Press, 1967.

The Songs and Sonets of John Donne. An *editio minor* with introduction and explanatory notes by Theodore Redpath. London: Methuen, 1956.

Biathanatos. Edited by M. Rudick and M. Pabst Battin. New York: Garland, 1985.

Devotions upon Emergent Occasions. Edited by John Sparrow with a bibliographical note by Geoffrey Keynes. Cambridge: Cambridge University Press, 1923.

Essays in Divinity. Edited by Evelyn M. Simpson. Oxford: Clarendon Press, 1952.

Ignatius His Conclave. Edited by T. S. Healy. Oxford: Clarendon Press, 1969.

The Sermons of John Donne. Edited with introductions and critical apparatus by George R. Potter and Evelyn M. Simpson. 10 vols. 1953–62. Reprint. Berkeley and Los Angeles: University of California Press, 1984.

The Complete Poetry and Selected Prose. Edited with an introduction by Charles M. Coffin. New York: Random House, 1952.

John Donne's Poetry: Authoritative Texts, Criticism. Selected and edited by A. L. Clements. New York: Norton, 1952.

Poetry and Prose. Edited by F. J. Warnke. New York: Random House, 1967.

SECONDARY SOURCES

Alvarez, A. *The School of Donne.* London: Chatto & Windus, 1961. Study
of Donne and the other Metaphysical poets in their social and cultural
setting, flawed by some erroneous historical assumptions.

Andreasen, N. J. C. *John Donne: Conservative Revolutionary.* Princeton:
Princeton University Press, 1967. A highly moralistic and ultimately
unpersuasive reading of Donne's love poetry.

Bald, R. C. *Donne's Influence in English Literature.* Morpeth, England: St.
John's College Press, 1932. Reprint. Gloucester, Mass.: Peter Smith,
1965). A thorough and scholarly examination of the subject.

————. *John Donne: A Life.* Edited by Wesley Milgate. New York and Oxford: Oxford University Press, 1970. Now the definitive biography of
Donne.

Bennett, Joan. *Four Metaphysical Poets: Donne, Herbert, Vaughan, Crashaw.*
1934. 2d. rev. ed. Cambridge: Cambridge University Press, 1957. Sensitive critical readings of Donne and some important contemporaries
and successors.

————. "The Love Poetry of John Donne. A Reply to Mr. C. S. Lewis."
In *Seventeenth-Century Studies Presented to Sir Herbert Grierson.* Oxford:
Clarendon Press, 1938. A defense of Donne's love poems against stric-
tures leveled by Lewis.

Bredvold, Louis I. "The Naturalism of Donne in Relation to Some Renaissance Traditions." *Journal of English and Germanic Philology* 22
(1923):471–502. A learned investigation of Donne's relationship to
some contemporaneous philosophical movements.

————. "The Religious Thought of Donne in Relation to Medieval and
Later Traditions." In *Studies in Shakespeare, Milton and Donne,* 191–232.
New York: Macmillan Co., 1925. Like the previous item, a very eru-
dite study of Donne's ideas.

Brooke, Rupert. "John Donne." *Poetry and Drama* 1 (1913):185–88. An
impressionistic but very lively essay standing near the beginning of the
twentieth-century rehabilitation of Donne's reputation.

Carey, John. *John Donne: Life, Mind, and Art.* London and New York: Oxford University Press, 1981. An important recent study—controversial
to some degree—of Donne's life and art. Lays much stress on the poet's
Catholic background.

Coffin, Charles Monroe. *John Donne and the New Philosophy.* 1937. Reprint.
New York: Columbia University Press, 1958. An early but still largely
valid assessment of the impact on Donne of the scientific revolution.

Colie, Rosalie L. *Paradoxia Epidemica: The Renaissance Tradition of Paradox.*
Princeton: Princeton University Press, 1966. Examines the mode of

paradox in Renaissance and baroque literature, with significant attention paid to Donne's work.

Cruttwell, Patrick. *The Shakespearean Moment and Its Place in the Poetry of the 17th Century.* London: Chatto & Windus, 1954. Attempts to isolate and identify the peculiar genius of early seventeenth-century literature.

Denonain, Jean-Jacques. *Thèmes et formes de la poésie "métaphysique": Étude d'un aspect de la littérature anglaise au dix-septième siècle.* Paris: Presses universitaires de France, 1956. An incisive study of the poetic movement of which Donne is the chief figure.

Duncan, Joseph E. *The Revival of Metaphysical Poetry: The History of a Style, 1800 to the Present.* Minneapolis: University of Minnesota Press, 1959. Traces in detail the critical rehabilitation of Donne and the other Metaphysicals.

Eliot, T. S. "Deux Attitudes Mystiques: Dante et Donne." Translated by Jean de Menasce. In *Le Roseau d'Or, Oeuvres et Chroniques,* 14, no. 3 (1927):149–73. The Anglo-American poet and critic examines two of the predecessors most important to his own development.

_____. "The Metaphysical Poets." *Times Literary Supplement,* 20 October 1921, 669–70. Reprint. In *Selected Essays.* New York: Harcourt, Brace, 1950. An enormously influential essay, crucial to the formation of critical attitudes toward Donne in the twentieth century.

Ellrodt, Robert. *L'Inspiration personnelle et l'esprit du temps chez les poètes métaphysiques anglais.* Paris: José Corti, 1960. Perhaps the most detailed and authoritative large study of Donne and the other Metaphysicals as a whole.

Fausset, Hugh L'Anson. *John Donne: A Study in Discord.* London: Jonathan Cape, 1924. An early critical biography, sometimes unreliable. Superseded by Bald.

Ferry, Anne. *All in War with Time: Love Poetry of Shakespeare, Donne, Jonson, Marvell.* Cambridge, Mass.: Harvard University Press, 1975. An insightful study of the love poetry of Donne and others.

Fiore, Peter Amadeus, ed., *Just So Much Honor: Essays Commemorating the Four-Hundredth Anniversary of the Birth of John Donne.* University Park, Pa.: Pennsylvania State University Press, 1972. Critical essays by various hands.

Gardner, Helen, ed. *John Donne: A Collection of Critical Essays.* 1962. Reprint. Englewood Cliffs, N.J.: Prentice Hall, 1963. Another collection of critical essays, some of them excellent, by diverse critics.

Granquist, Raoul. *The Reputation of John Donne, 1779–1873.* Uppsala, Sweden: Almquist & Wiksell, 1975. A very detailed and careful study of Donne's reputation.

Guss, Donald L. *John Donne, Petrarchist: Italianate Conceits and Love Theory in the Songs and Sonnets.* Detroit: Wayne State University Press, 1966.

Reassesses the relation of Donne to Petrarch and the entire Petrarchan tradition and contends, convincingly, that the relation was more important and more positive than generally acknowledged.

Harris, Victor. *All Coherence Gone*. Chicago: University of Chicago Press, 1949. Another study of Donne in relation to the disturbing scientific ideas of his time.

Hester, M. Thomas. *Kinde Pitty and Brave Scorn*. Durham, N.C.: Duke University Press, 1982. A study of the *satyres*.

Hughes, Merritt, Y. "'Kidnapping Donne." *University of California Publications in English,* 4 (1934):61–89. A scholar's refutation of contemporaneous attempts to make Donne a kind of twentieth-century man and artist. Asserts the importance of understanding his connections with his own time.

———. "The Lineage of 'The Extasie.' " *Modern Language Review* 27 (1932):1–5. An erudite interpretation of one of Donne's most controversial love poems, in the light of Renaissance tradition.

Hunt, Clay. *Donne's Poetry: Essays in Literary Analysis*. New Haven, Conn.: Yale University Press, 1954. Shrewd and often persuasive explications of several of Donne's major poems.

Husain, Itrat. *The Dogmatic and Mystical Theology of John Donne*. With a preface by Sir Herbert J. C. Grierson. New York: Macmillan Co. 1938. An important study of Donne's religious thought.

Jackson, Robert S. *John Donne's Christian Vocation*. Evanston: Northwestern University Press, 1970. Another study of Donne's religion.

John Donne Journal: Studies in the Age of Donne. Edited by M. Thomas Hester and R. V. Young. Raleigh, N.C. 1982–. A recently founded journal concerned with Donne and his age.

Keynes, Geoffrey. *Bibliography of the Works of Dr. John Donne. Dean of St. Paul's*. Cambridge: Baskerville Club, 1914. 2d ed. 1932. 3d ed. 1958. An essential tool for Donne scholars.

Legouis, Pierre. *Donne the Craftsman: An Essay upon the Structure of the Songs and Sonnets*. Paris: Henri Didier, 1928. A lively and often controversial study of Donne's love poetry, including a reading of "The Extasie" radically opposed to the readings of Hughes and others.

Leishman, J. B. *The Metaphysical Poets: Donne, Herbert, Vaughan, Traherne*. Oxford: Clarendon Press, 1934. One of the best general studies of Donne and his followers in the Metaphysical succession.

———. *The Monarch of Wit: An Analytical and Comparative Study of the Poetry of John Donne*. London: Hutchinson University Library, 1951. Rev. ed. London: Hillery, 1962. An excellent all-around study of the poetry.

Lewalski, Barbara Kiefer. *Donne's "Anniversaries" and the Poetry of Praise: The Creation of a Symbolic Mode*. Princeton: Princeton University Press, 1973. An essential volume for the serious study of Donne's most ambitious and difficult poems.

_____. *Protestant Poetics and the Seventeenth-Century Religious Lyric.* Princeton: Princeton University Press, 1979. A revisionist study that places the religious poetry of Donne and others in a specifically Protestant context as opposed to the general context of Continental Catholicism in which he is placed by Martz and others.

Lewis, C. S. "Donne and Love Poetry in the Seventeenth Century." In *Seventeenth-Century Studies Presented to Sir Herbert Grierson.* Oxford: Clarendon Press, 1938. A largely negative assessment of Donne's love poetry. Refutation provided by Joan Bennett.

Martz, Louis L. *The Poem of the Mind: Essays on Poetry, English and American.* New York: Oxford University Press, 1966. Essays on various English and American poets, including Donne.

_____. *The Poetry of Meditation: A Study in English Religious Literature of the Seventeenth Century.* 1954. Rev. ed. New Haven, Conn.: Yale University Press, 1962. Of great importance, a seminal work for the study not only of Donne but of all seventeenth-century religious poetry. Relates that poetry to the devotional practice of formal meditation.

_____. *The Wit of Love: Donne, Carew, Crashaw, Marvell.* Notre Dame, Ind.: University of Notre Dame Press, 1969. Further reflections on Donne and his contemporaries.

McKevlin, Dennis. *A Lecture in Love's Philosophy: Donne's Vision of the World of Human Love in the Songs and Sonets.* Lanham, Md.: University Press of America, 1984. Another study of Donne's love lyrics.

Miner, Earl. *The Metaphysical Mode from Donne to Cowley.* Princeton: Princeton University Press, 1969. A perceptive analysis of the style of the Metaphysical poets, with much attention, of course, to Donne.

Mitchell, W. Fraser. *English Pulpit Oratory from Andrewes to Tillotson: A Study of Its Literary Aspects.* London: Society for Promoting Christian Knowledge, 1932. An important study of the subject, with appropriate attention dedicated to Donne.

Moloney, Michael Francis. *John Donne: His Flight from Mediaevalism.* Illinois Studies in Language and Literature, vol. 29, nos. 2–3. Urbana: University of Illinois Press, 1944. A relatively early study of Donne's reaction to his intellectual heritage.

Mueller, William R. *John Donne: Preacher.* Princeton: Princeton University Press, 1962. An examination of Donne as pulpit orator.

Nicolson, Marjorie Hope. *The Breaking of the Circle.* Evanston: Northwestern University Press, 1950. Rev. ed. New York: Columbia University Press, 1960. A very important study of the English poetic imagination in its response to the scientific revolution, with Donne figuring very conspicuously.

Praz, Mario. *Secentismo e marinismo in Inghilterra: John Donne-Richard Crashaw.* Florence, Italy: La Voce, 1925. A pioneering study in analogies between Donne (and his English contemporaries) and comparable phenomena in Italy.

Ramsey, Mary Paton. *Les Doctrines médiévales chez Donne, le poète métaphysicien de l'Angleterre (1573–1631).* London: Oxford University Press, 1917. One of the very earliest studies of Donne in relation to his medieval patrimony. Still important.

Roberts, John R. *John Donne: An Annotated Bibliography of Modern Criticism, 1912–1967.* Columbia: University of Missouri Press, 1973. Like its sequel (see below), an indispensable tool for the scholar.

————. *John Donne: An Annotated Bibliography of Modern Criticism: 1968–1978.* Columbia: University of Missouri Press, 1979.

Roston, Murray. *The Soul of Wit: A Study of John Donne.* Oxford: Clarendon Press, 1974. One of the many examinations of one of the most salient aspects of Donne's genius.

Rugoff, Milton Allan. *Donne's Imagery: A Study in Creative Sources.* New York: Corporate, 1939. Reprint. New York: Russell & Russell, 1962. An examination of Donne's images, in terms of the quantitative method in favor during the 1930s.

Sharp, Robert Lathrop. *From Donne to Dryden: The Revolt against Metaphysical Poetry.* Chapel Hill: University of North Carolina Press, 1940. An historical study of the emergence of Augustan style after the deterioration of the Metaphysical style best exemplified in Donne's work.

Sherwood, Terry G. *Fulfilling the Circle: A Study of John Donne's Thought.* Toronto: University of Toronto Press, 1984. A recent study, exemplifying the serious attention that continues to be given to Donne, as thinker as well as poet and prose artist.

Simpson, Evelyn M. *A Study of the Prose Works of John Donne.* Oxford: Clarendon Press, 1924. A central and still authoritative work for the study of Donne's prose.

Smith, A. J., ed. *John Donne: Essays in Celebration.* London: Methuen, 1972. A fairly recent collection of appreciative and often informative essays by various hands.

Smith, James. "On Metaphysical Poetry." *Scrutiny* 2 (1934):222–39. One of the most perceptive and probing theoretical considerations of the poetic style best exemplified in England by Donne.

Spencer, Theodore, ed. *A Garland for John Donne, 1631–1931.* Cambridge, Mass.: Harvard University Press, 1931. Essays by various hands. Exemplary for the formalist approach current in the 1930s.

Stampfer, Judah. *John Donne and the Metaphysical Gesture.* New York: Funk & Wagnalls, 1970. A relatively late example of the conception of Donne's work as exhibiting a special value for the modern reader.

Stein, Arnold. *John Donne's Lyrics: The Eloquence of Action.* Minneapolis: University of Minnesota Press, 1962. An intensely detailed, very original, and often brilliant study of Donne's lyric work, both amorous and devotional.

Unger, Leonard. *Donne's Poetry and Modern Criticism.* Chicago: Henry Regnery, 1950. Considers, most appropriately, the special privileging of Donne's work in the theory and criticism of the early and middle twentieth century.

Warnke, Frank J., ed. *European Metaphysical Poetry.* New Haven, Conn.: Yale University Press, 1961. An anthology of translations from Continental poetry. Attempts to demonstrate the presence elsewhere in Europe of the kind of poetry exemplified in England by Donne's work.

_____. *Versions of Baroque: European Literature in the Seventeenth Century.* New Haven, Conn.: Yale University Press, 1972. A more detailed study, viewing the Metaphysical style in poetry and prose as a variant of the baroque and illustrating frequently with reference to Donne's work.

Webber, Joan. *Contrary Music: The Prose Style of John Donne.* Madison: University of Wisconsin Press, 1963. One of the best and most helpful studies of Donne's style as a prose writer.

_____. *The Eloquent "I": Style and Self in Seventeenth-Century Prose.* Madison: University of Wisconsin Press, 1968. A broader study, but one that still has much to say about Donne as prose artist.

White, Helen C. *The Metaphysical Poets: A Study in Religious Experience.* New York: Macmillan Co., 1936. Reprint. New York: Collier Books, 1962. One of the monuments of the earlier twentieth-century fascination with Donne and his poetic contemporaries. Retains much of its value, especially with reference to Donne's religious poetry.

Williamson, George. *The Donne Tradition: A Study in English Poetry from Donne to the Death of Cowley.* Cambridge, Mass.: Harvard University Press, 1930. Like the White study, an example of earlier twentieth-century special enthusiasm. This work displays—and generously admits—a particular debt to T. S. Eliot.

_____. *Seventeenth-Century Contexts.* London: Faber & Faber, 1960. A collection of later essays by a master of seventeenth-century English studies. Many of them are concerned with Donne.

Index